内蒙古财经大学实训与案例教材系列丛书

丛书主编　金　桩　徐全忠

会计学原理案例双语教程

主编　孙鹏云

中国财经出版传媒集团

经济科学出版社
Economic Science Press

图书在版编目（CIP）数据

会计学原理案例双语教程：英文、汉文/孙鹏云主编.
—北京：经济科学出版社，2020.6
（内蒙古财经大学实训与案例教材系列丛书）
ISBN 978-7-5218-1667-9

Ⅰ.①会…　Ⅱ.①孙…　Ⅲ.①会计学-案例-双语教学-高等学校-教材-英、汉　Ⅳ.①F230

中国版本图书馆 CIP 数据核字（2020）第 112818 号

责任编辑：于海汛　李　林
责任校对：刘　昕
责任印制：李　鹏　范　艳

会计学原理案例双语教程
主编　孙鹏云
经济科学出版社出版、发行　新华书店经销
社址：北京市海淀区阜成路甲 28 号　邮编：100142
总编部电话：010-88191217　发行部电话：010-88191522
网址：www.esp.com.cn
电子邮件：esp@esp.com.cn
天猫网店：经济科学出版社旗舰店
网址：http://jjkxcbs.tmall.com
北京密兴印刷有限公司印装
787×1092　16 开　10.75 印张　230000 字
2020 年 10 月第 1 版　2020 年 10 月第 1 次印刷
ISBN 978-7-5218-1667-9　定价：46.00 元
（图书出现印装问题，本社负责调换。电话：010-88191510）

前　言

编者在参考了国外的相关文献和国内相关教材后，按照会计循环的流程，构建了本书的基本结构。本书共分七章，第一章概述会计作为商业语言的特性，第二章叙述利用会计恒等式分析经济业务的方法，第三章阐释复式记账法及T型账的用法，第四章介绍日记账与分类账的登记方法，第五章叙述账项调整与工作底稿的运用，第六章涉及结账分录与结账后试算平衡表的编制，第七章梳理会计重要概念与原则，将会计实务与理论紧密结合起来。

本书主要讲解会计学的基本理论、基本方法以及基本流程，并结合各章主要专业术语的中英文对照，使初学者全面学习会计专业知识，满足对外交流和使用的需要。本书章节中设有自测题，每章后附有思考题和练习题，帮助读者测试其对专业知识掌握和应用的情况；章节中还设有“知识点解析”“小提示”，帮助读者提高理解与分析能力；各章后的扩展阅读和案例分析有助于读者进一步拓宽视野，提升文献阅读能力。

本书用语简洁规范，可作为会计双语教学的教材，也可作为高等院校学生的参考书和从事国际会计业务人员的学习书籍，其他会计从业人员、管理人员、审计和税务人员等也可用作阅读材料。

由于编者水平有限和时间仓促，书中的疏漏及错误在所难免，恳请读者批评指正。

编　者

2019年8月

目 录
CONTENTS

CHAPTER 1 An Introduction to Accounting 会计概述

本章学习目标

1. 理解会计的内涵。
2. 了解会计领域的职业机会。
3. 能够列举财务信息的主要使用者。
4. 了解企业主体的三种不同类型的组织形式及其异同。

本章核心术语

accounting 会计
accounting system 会计系统
auditing 审计
auditor's report 审计报告
Certified Public Accountant（CPA） 注册会计师
corporation 公司
creditor 债权人
economic entity 经济主体
entity 主体
financial statements 财务报表
governmental accounting 政府会计
management advisory services 管理咨询服务
partnership 合伙制
public accountants 公共会计师
separate entity assumption 会计主体假设
social entity 社会主体
sole proprietorship 个人独资（单人业主制）

stockholders 股东

tax accounting 税务会计

The purpose of accounting is to provide financial information about a business or a nonprofit organization. This information is of interest to owners, managers and other parties outside the business or nonprofit organization. Since accounting is used to gather and communicate financial information, it is often called the "language of business".

1.1 Accounting Defined 会计的含义

Accounting is the process by which financial information about a business is recorded, classified, summarized, interpreted and communicated to owners, managers and other interested parties. An **accounting system** is designed to accumulate data about a firm's financial affairs, classify the data in a meaningful way, and summarize it in periodic reports called **financial statements**. Owners and managers receive much of the information they need from financial statements. The accountant not only establishes the records and procedures that make up the accounting system and supervises the operations of the system but also interprets the resulting financial information. Most owners and managers rely heavily on the accountant's judgment and knowledge when making financial decisions.

1.2 Fields of Accounting 会计领域

The field of accounting is divided into three broad divisions: public, private and governmental accounting. Many jobs are available in accounting, and they require varying amounts of education and experience.

1.2.1 Public Accounting

Public accounting is the field of accounting that provides a variety of accounting services to clients for a fee. Professional accountants belong to firms whose major business is the performance of accounting services for other companies. These firms are called public accounting firms. They offer three major types of services: auditing, tax accounting, and management advisory services.

知识点解析：

public accounting 公共会计。公共会计是指注册会计师提供的审计、会计和税务服务等。近年来，在公共会计中，企业管理咨询业务迅速发展，占公共会计组织业务收入的比重相当大。

Many professional accountants who works in a public accounting firm usually are **certified public accountants (CPAs)**. To become a CPA, an individual must have earned a certain number of college credits in accounting courses, demonstrate good personal character, pass the Uniform CPA Examination, and fulfill the experience requirements of the state of practice.

知识点解析：

Certified Public Accountant（CPA）注册会计师。指有资格执行审计业务的专业人员，一般需要满足三个方面的条件才能获得这种资格：(1) 接受过专业教育，通常要有本科学历，有的国家甚至要求更高的学历；(2) 具有一定期间的会计或审计工作经验；(3) 通过由会计专业团体举办的统一考试。注册会计师在英联邦国家也称特许会计师，即 Chartered Accountants（CA）。

A CPA is an independent accountant who provides accounting services to the public. So CPAs must also have an independent mental attitude. Independence can not be absolute by any means, but it must be a goal that is worked toward, and it can be achieved to a certain degree. CPAs may not be sufficiently independent if they are also company employees.

知识点解析：

independent mental attitude 独立的精神态度，是对注册会计师的超然独立性的要求。注册会计师的超然独立性是做出客观公正的审计结论的首要条件，因此，它往往被看作是审计理论和审计实务的基石。如果注册会计师没有独立性，那么审计结论就是不可信的。

Auditing is the review of financial statements to assess their fairness and adherence to accounting standards. Auditing is performed by auditors who are CPAs. Tax accounting is a service offered by public accounting firms that involves tax compliance and tax planning. Tax compliance is any activity associated with the preparation of tax returns and the audit of those returns. **Tax planning** involves giving advice to clients on how to legally structure their financial affairs to reduce their tax liability. Providing **management advisory services** involves helping clients improve their information systems or improve their business performance.

知识点解析：

auditing 审计。审计主要有三种类型：经营审计、合规性审计和财务报表审计。

operational audit 经营审计。经营审计是为了评价被审计单位的经营活动，对其经营程序和方法中的任何一个部分进行检查和评价，并向其管理当局提出改进的建议。经营审计的主要目的是评价经营的效率和效果，而不是评价会计报表的公允性。

compliance audit 合规性审计。合规性审计是为了检查和确定被审计单位的经济活动是否符合国家法律和有关部门制定的条例和合同条款的规定而进行的审计。例如，审查一个企业或个人是否遵守了税法，依法填报纳税申报单。

audit of financial statements 财务报表审计。财务报表审计是为了确定被审计单位的财务报表是否符合特定的标准而进行的审计。正常情况下，这种特定的标准就是一般公认会计原则，尽管财务报表审计也包括对按收付实现制或其他适用的会计基础编制的财务报表的审计。

1.2.2 Private Accounting

Private accounting involves working on the staff of a single business in industry. Private accountants perform a wide range of activities. They establish a company's accounting policies, direct its accounting system, prepare its financial statements, interpret its financial information, and provide financial advice to management. In addition, private accountants prepare tax forms, perform tax planning services for the company, and prepare internal reports for management.

1.2.3 Governmental Accounting

Governmental accounting involves keeping financial records and preparing financial reports as part of the staff of governmental units. Although governmental units do not earn profits, they receive and pay out huge amounts of money and must have procedures for recording and managing this money.

Test your understanding

The main purpose of financial accounting is to (   ).

A. record all transactions in the books of account

B. provide management with detailed analyses of cost

C. enable preparation of financial statements that provide information about an entity's financial performance and position

D. calculate profit or loss for an accounting period

1.3 Users of Financial Information 财务信息的使用者

The result of the accounting process are communicated to many individuals and organizations who are interested in the financial affairs of a business. Who are these individuals and organizations, and why might they want to obtain financial information about a particular firm?

1.3.1 Managers

Managers of a business need the most information, to help them make their planning and control decisions. They obviously have "special" access to information about the business, because they are able to demand whatever internally produced statements they require. Management is also responsible for producing the financial statements.

小提示：

请注意，编制财务报表是企业管理层的职责，管理层有责任确保其财务报表是真实公允的。审计师只对财务报表进行鉴证并发表合适的审计意见，编制财务报表不应该由审计师来负责。

1.3.2 Investors

Investors and potential investors are interested in their potential profits and the security of their investment. Future profits may be estimated from the target company's past performance as shown in the income statement. The security of their investment will be revealed by the financial strength and solvency of the company as shown in the balance sheet.

1.3.3 Suppliers

Even though your business is small, a number of people other than you, the owner, may be interested in its financial affairs. For example, when you first ask for credit from suppliers of goods, they may want financial information in order to assess the ability of your firm to pay its debts. They may also use the data to determine exactly how much credit you should be given.

1.3.4 Banks

What if you decide to ask your bank for a loan so that you can open a new store across town? The bank will want to assure itself that your firm will pay back the loan in a timely fashion. The bank will therefore require that you provide financial information prepared by your accountant and will use this information in determining whether to give you the loan and in setting the terms of the loan.

1.3.5 Customers

In some industries customers pay special attention to financial information about the firm with which they plan to do business. They may use this information to try to estimate how long the company will be operating. The computer industry is an example of one where customers are concerned about the life of a firm. Before a customer spends a lot of money on a computer, that customer will want to feel reasonably sure that the manufacturer will be around for the next several years to service the computer, replace parts and provide additional components. Also, the customer will want to be able to purchase programs for that computer as the need arises. If the computer manufacturer goes out of business, it is likely that programmers and software houses will stop writing programs to fit that manufacturer's computer. One way the customer can estimate the economic health of a company and the likelihood that it will remain in business is by analyzing financial information about the firm.

1.3.6 Employees

Employees may also be interested in having financial information about the business where they work. For example, they may be members of a profit-sharing plan and therefore be very concerned about the financial results of the firm's operations. If a large corporation has employees who belong to a labor union, the union may use financial information about the firm to assess its ability to pay higher wages and benefits when a new contract is negotiated.

Test your understanding

Which of the following best explains why employees are interested in the financial statements of their employer?

A. To compare the business with its competitor in order to seek employment with one of those competitors

B. To assess the effect of the business on the local economy, community and environment

C. To assess whether the business will continue into the foreseeable future

D. To assess the profitability of the business in order to decide whether to invest in it

1.3.7 Government Agencies

Government agencies need to know how the economy is performing in order to plan financial and industrial policies. So they are interested in the allocation of resources and therefore in the activities of business entities. They also require information in order to provide a basis for national statistics. The taxation authorities want to know about business profits in order to assess the tax payable by the company, including sales taxes.

1.3.8 The Public

The public may wish to assess the effect of the company on the economy, local environment and local community. Companies may contribute to their local economy and community through providing employment and patronizing local suppliers. Some companies also run corporate responsibility programmes through which they support the environment, economy and community by, for example supporting recycling schemes.

Test your understanding

Which of the following users do you think require the most detailed financial information to be made available to them?

A. competitors

B. management of the business

C. trade unions

D. investors

1.4 Types of Business Entities 企业主体的组织形式

The accounting process involves recording, classifying, summarizing, interpreting and communicating financial information about an economic or social entity. An **entity** is something that can be recognized as having its own separate identity, such as an individual, a town, a university, or a business. The term **economic entity** usually refers to a business or organization whose major purpose is to produce a profit for its owners. **Social entities** are nonprofit organizations, such as cities, public schools and public hospitals. This book focuses on the accounting process for businesses, although nonprofit organizations need similar financial information.

知识点解析：

business entity 即 accounting entity，企业主体即会计主体。会计主体指会计工作为其服务的特定单位或组织，为“谁”服务，“谁”就是会计主体。需要注意的是，会计主体与法律主体不同，一般来说，法律主体一定是会计主体，但会计主体不一定是法律主体。

There are three major legal forms of business entity: the sole proprietorship, the partnership and the corporation. While the accounting process for all three types of business entity is generally the same, differences in their structures and in the laws that apply to these structures require some differences in the way certain aspects of their financial affairs are recorded. However, for now you should understand the basic differences in the three types of business entities.

Test your understanding

which of the following statements defines the business entity concept?

A. The business will continue to operate for the foreseeable future

B. The business is always a separate legal entity, distinct from those who own or manage that business

C. The business is never a separate legal entity from those who own or manage that business

D. Financial transactions are recorded and presented from the perspective of the business, rather than from the perspective of the owners or managers of that business

1.4.1 Sole Proprietorship

A **sole proprietorship** is a business entity owned by one person. The life of the business ends when the owner is no longer willing or able to keep the firm going. Many small businesses are operated as sole proprietorships.

The owner of a sole proprietorship is legally responsible for the debts and taxes of the business. If, for example, the firm is unable to pay its debts, the **creditors** (those people, companies, or government agencies to whom the firm owes money) can turn to the owner for payment. The owner may then have to pay the debts of the business from personal savings or other personal resources. When the time comes to pay income taxes, the owner's income and the income of the business are combined to compute the total tax responsibility of the owner.

知识点解析：

sole proprietorship 个人独资，独资企业，又称 proprietorship 或 single proprietorship。企业的一种组织形式，是由一个人拥有和管理的企业。在西方，指企业的净资产归一个所有者所有的企业。独资企业具有设立容易、免征企业所得税和较少受法律约束的优点，其缺点是融资能力有限、发展能力有限、所有者对企业的债务负无限责任。独资企业不属于独立法人组织，但从会计角度来说，独资企业是独立的会计主体。

While the owner's money and the money of the business may seem to be almost the same, it is very important that the accounting process for the business be limited to the financial transactions of the firm. Remember, accounting deals with financial information about an economic entity. If the owner's personal transactions are mixed up with those of the business, it will be very difficult to measure the performance of the firm. Accountants use the term **separate entity assumption** to describe this idea of separating the accounting process for a business from the accounting process for the personal finances of the owner or owners.

Test your understanding

If a car dealer takes a new car from inventory for his own personal use, which of the following accounting concept should be considered?

A. the faithful presentation concept

B. the accruals concept

C. the going concern concept

D. the business entity concept

1.4.2 Partnerships

A **partnership** is a business entity owned by two or more people. The partnership structure is common in businesses that offer a professional service, such as law firms, accounting firms, architectural firms, medical practices and dental practices. At the beginning of the partnership, two or more individuals enter into a contract that outlines how much each partner will contribute to the business; each partner's percentage of ownership; what share of the profits which partner will receive; what duties each partner will perform; how much responsibility each partner will have to creditors and tax authorities for the amounts owed by business; and other information detailing the rights, obligations and limitations of each partner. The partner may share equally in the ownership and profits of the business, or they may share in any proportion agreed upon in the contract. When an individual is unwilling or unable to remain a partner, then the partnership dissolves and a new partnership may be formed with the remaining partners or with new partners.

知识点解析：

partnership合伙企业，是企业的一种组织形式。两个或更多的人以书面约定为基础，合并他们的资产组成一个企业，并分享企业的收益或分担损失。在西方，成立合伙企业不需要经过法律程序，也不需要缴纳企业所得税。合伙人对企业的债务负无限责任，合伙人之间存在相互代理关系，这一点要求在成立合伙企业时要谨慎选择合伙人。从会计角度说，合伙企业也是独立的会计主体。

As in a sole proprietorship, the partners are individually, and as a group, responsible for the debts and taxes of the partnership. Their personal bank or other personal resources may be used to pay creditors when the partnership is unable to provide payment. Again, it is important that the accounting process for a partnership be limited to the financial transactions of the firm and not include the personal transactions of the partners.

Test your understanding

Which one of the following statements regarding partnerships is correct?

A. The partners' individual exposure to debt is limited

B. Financial statements for the partnership by law must be produced and made public

C. A partnership is not a separate legal entity from the partners themselves

D. A partnership makes raising finance easier because additional shares can be issued to raise additional cash

1.4.3 Corporations

A **corporation** is a business entity that is separate from its owners and has a legal right to own property and do business in its own name. The corporation is considerably different from the other business entities—the sole proprietorship and the partnership. The major difference has to do with the ownership of the business. There are publicly owned and privately owned corporations. Anyone can invest in a publicly owned corporation. The stock represents ownership in a corporation and is issued as stock certificates.

The corporate form of business entity is unique in that the firm does not end when ownership changes—as through the sale of shares of stock by one individual to another. Some corporations have new owners daily because their shares are actively traded on stock exchanges. One of the advantages of a corporation is that it can last forever, whereas the maximum life of a sole proprietorship is the life of its owner. Similarly, a partnership can last only as long as the life span of any of its partners. The death or withdrawal of one partner ends the partnership.

知识点解析：

corporation 公司、股份公司，是企业组织形式的一种。公司的优点是可以筹集大额资金，所有者的责任有限，股权容易转移。缺点是税负重，必须接受政府更严格的监管。公司的成立需要经过政府批准，要有公司章程并根据公司章程从事融资和经营活动。公司是独立于所有者的法律主体，要缴纳企业所得税。

Corporate owners, often called **stockholders**, or *shareholders*, are not responsible for the debts or taxes of the corporation. The most money a stockholder can lose if the corporation is unable to pay its bills is the total of his or her investment in the firm—the cost of the shares of stock purchased and held by the stockholder.

Test your understanding

Which one of the following statements is true?

A. The director of a company are liable for any losses of the company

B. A sole proprietorship is owned by shareholders and operated by the proprietor

C. Partners are liable for debts in a partnership in proportion to their profit share ratio

D. A corporation is run by directors on behalf of its members

1.5 Auditor's Report 审计报告

The financial statements must be audited, or reviewed, by an accountant who is not on the staff of the firm that issued the statements, that is, by an independent certified public accountant to ensure accounting standards are followed by publicly owned corporations. In addition, the financial statements must include a report by the accountant about the review. This document is known as the **auditor's report**. The purpose of the review is to obtain the objective opinion of a professional accountant from outside the company that the financial statements fairly present the operating results and financial position of the business and that the information was prepared according to accounting standards. The financial statements and the auditor's report must be made available to stockholders and potential stockholders of publicly owned corporations.

知识点解析：

auditor's report 审计报告。审计报告是注册会计师发布的关于被审计单位财务报表是否公允的书面文件，审计报告通常涉及4种审计意见（auditor's opinion）：无保留意见、保留意见、拒绝表示意见、否定意见。

unqualified opinion 无保留意见。在能够确认财务报表的编制符合会计准则的要求，并公允地反映了被审计单位的财务状况、经营成果和现金流量的情况下表示的审计意见。

qualified opinion 保留意见。指注册会计师对财务报表的反映有所保留的审计意见。注册会计师认为财务报表的反映就整体而言是恰当的，但是存在个别会计事项的处理违背了会计准则，或审计范围受到了局部限制等情况，一般会表示保留意见。

disclaimer of opinion 拒绝表示意见。当注册会计师在审计过程中，由于审计范围受到严重限制，无法获得必要的证据，以至无法对财务报表整体发表意见时，表示的审计意见。

adverse opinion 否定意见。当注册会计师认为财务报表严重违背会计准则，严重歪曲了财务状况、经营成果和现金流量，且被审计单位拒绝调整时，可表示否定意见。

Businesses and the environment in which they operate are constantly changing. The economy, technology and laws change. Therefore, financial information and the methods of presenting that information must change to meet the needs of the people who use the information. Accounting standards are changed and refined as accountants respond to the changing environment.

本章小结：

会计是对财务信息进行记录、分类、汇总并报告的一个过程，为企业的所有者、管理者和其他所有利益相关者服务。会计通常有三个主要领域：公共会计、管理会计和政府会计。

独资企业、合伙企业和公司制企业具有不同的组织结构和运营规则，税务和监管机构的要求各有不同，但在都需要财务信息这一点上是相同的。非营利组织和政府机构也同样需要财务信息，以便更高效地开展工作。

财务会计为“对外会计”，为保证会计信息的有用性，要求其必须遵循会计准则。为了保护公众利益，审计师的审计意见尤为重要。

Self－Review & Questions 自测题

1. What are the three types of business entities?
2. What is the separate entity assumption, and why is it important in accounting for a business?
3. Who are the internal and external users of accounting information?
4. What are the differences among the public accounting, governmental accounting and private accounting?
5. Explain how does each group of information users apply accounting information.
6. What is the purpose of accounting?
7. Why is accounting called “the language of business”?
8. What dose the accounting process involve?
9. What are financial statements?

Translations 翻译题

Translate the following English into Chinese or Chinese into English.

1. Owners, managers, creditors, banks, and many others use the financial statements to make decisions about the business.
2. The managers of a business must make sure that the firm has an efficient accounting

system that produces financial information that is timely, accurate, and fair.

3. Internal reports for management need not follow the accounting principles but should provide useful information that will aid in the process of monitoring and controlling operations.

4. When properly studied and interpreted, financial information can help managers do a more effective job of controlling present operations, making decisions, and planning for the future.

5. All types of business need and use financial information. Nonprofit organizations also need similar types of financial information in order to conduct their operations in an efficient manner.

6. 管理政府事务也需要利用会计来对政府的运作进行记录、计划和控制。

7. 会计信息外部使用者不直接参与经营管理，我们所有的人几乎都使用会计信息。

8. 管理会计主要为内部信息使用者提供决策所需要的信息，但内部报告所遵循的规则与外部报告不同。

Supplementary Reading　扩展阅读

Cost Accounting and Managerial Accounting

1. Cost Accounting

Cost accounting is an essential specialty within the accounting field. The main objective of industry is to determine the selling price of the products or the cost of services that are furnished by a company. The main concepts in cost accounting include: (1) direct materials, (2) indirect materials, (3) direct labor, (4) indirect labor, and (5) manufacturing overhead. Direct materials include all materials of an integral part of the finished product and are easily traced to the finished product. Indirect materials are used in the manufacturing process but are not easily traced to specific units or batches of production and are accounted for as factory overhead. The indirect materials don't enter into or become a part of the finished product. Direct labor represents the gross wages of personnel who worked directly on the production of goods. Indirect labor is used in the manufacturing process but is not applied to the finished product. Manufacturing overhead consists of costs except direct material and direct labor, including indirect materials, indirect labor, depreciation, electricity, fuel, insurance, and property taxes.

There are two principles of cost accounting systems. The first one is job-order cost accounting, which is suitable for use with the assembly type of manufacturing. It is used to determine the cost of an individual item or a batch, or job of lots of identical items. Under this costing system, the prime cost is the sum of direct material costs and direct labor costs. The completed products sold are reported as cost sold on the income statement, the unsold units are carried in the finished goods inventory account on the balance sheet. The second one is process cost accounting, which is suitable for use with the continuous process type of manufacturing. It is based on a time period that is usually determined by the nature of the processing.

2. Managerial Accounting

Managerial accounting is concerned with the provision of information to people within the organization to help them make better decisions. The decision-making process consists of seven stages: (1) identify objectives; (2) search for alternative courses of action; (3) gather information about alternatives; (4) select alternative courses of action; (5) implement the decisions; (6) compare actual and planned outcomes; (7) respond to variances from plan. The first five stages represent the planning process, involving making choices between alternatives. The final two stages represent the control process, including measuring and correcting actual performance to ensure that the alternatives are chosen and the plans for implementing them are carried out.

Management in a company consists of the following functions: (1) planning, (2) controlling, (3) organizing, (4) communicating and (5) motivating. In the planning process, the managerial accounting is to aid the management accounts to formulate future plans. In the controlling process, management accounting's function is to aid the control process by providing performance reports that compare the actual with the planned outcomes. In the organizing process, the managerial accounting is to aid the managers to assign the work to different people and make the people work efficiently. In the communicating process, the managerial accounting is to aid the communication function by installing and maintaining an effective communication and reporting system. In the motivating process, the managerial accounting is to help to set up a motivational system so that the employees can devote themselves to the work and have a high sincerity to the company.

CHAPTER 2 Analyzing Transactions 分析经济业务

本章学习目标

1. 分析经济业务对资产、负债和所有者权益的影响，并将其以会计等式的形式表示出来。
2. 掌握资产类账户、负债类账户和所有者权益类账户之间的关系。
3. 掌握会计等式中的数据如何呈现在利润表中。
4. 掌握会计等式中的数据如何呈现在所有者权益表和资产负债表中。

本章核心术语

accounts payable　应付账款
accounts receivable　应收账款
assets　资产
balance sheet　资产负债表
break even　保本点
business transaction　经济业务
capital　资本
equity　权益
expense　费用
fair market value　公允价值
fundamental accounting equation　基本会计等式（会计恒等式）
income statement　利润表
liabilities　负债
net income　净收益
net loss　净损失
on account　赊账，赊欠买卖

owner's equity　所有者权益（业主权益）
revenue　收入
statement of owner's equity　所有者权益表（业主权益表）
withdrawals　个人提款

Long before there can be any recording, reporting, or interpreting of financial information, accountants have to analyze every business transaction. A business transaction is a financial event that that changes the resources of the firm. A business transaction may consist of a purchase, a sale, a receipt or payment of cash, or any other financial occurrence. The effects of each transaction must be studied in order to know what information to record and where to record it.

The accounting process actually begins with an analysis of the transactions of a business; thus this phase is the natural starting point for the study of accounting.

知识点解析：

transactions 交易，也可称作事项（events）。是指影响企业的财务状况和经营成果的交易活动和事项，是会计核算的对象，因此会计循环的第一步就是要识别和记录交易和事项。

2.1　Beginning with Analysis　以分析为起点

Let's see how an accountant would analyze the transactions of Sun Financial Services, a firm that provides a wide range of bookkeeping and accounting services. This sole proprietorship business is owned by Sun Peng, who has a master's degree in accounting and is also a CPA. The office is managed by Zhang Hua, who has a bachelor's degree in accounting. The firm is located in a large office complex that has easy public access.

2.1.1　Starting a Business

Let's start from the beginning. Sun Peng obtained the funds to start the business by withdrawing ￥40 000 from his personal savings account. He deposited the money in a new bank account that he opened in the name of the firm, Sun Financial Services. The separate bank account for the firm helps Sun Peng keep his financial interest in the business separate from his personal funds. The establishment of this bank account on November 6, 20×8, was the first transaction of the new firm.

In setting up his accounting records, Sun Peng recognized that there were two important financial facts to be recorded at the time.

(1) The business had ¥40 000 of property in the form of cash, which was on deposit in the bank.

(2) Sun Peng had a ¥40 000 financial interest in the business; this interest is called his equity, or capital.

The firm's position at that time may be expressed as a simple equation (see Table 2 -1).

Table 2 -1 Starting a Business

	Property	=	Financial Interest
	Cash	=	Capital
(1) Invested cash	+40 000		
(2) Increased equity			+40 000

The equation *property equals financial interest* reflects the basic fact that in a free enterprise system all property is owned by someone. In this case Sun Peng owns the business because he supplied the property (cash).

知识点解析：

savings account 储蓄账户，又称 saving deposit，储蓄存款。是银行为小额储蓄存款所开设的账户，属于定期存款（time deposit）的一种。银行对储蓄存款账户支付利息，存款人在提取款项前，需提前通知银行，不允许使用支票当天取款。

2.1.2 Renting Facilities

The first thing Sun Peng did after setting up the business with his cash investment was to rent facilities. The lease he signed specified a monthly rent of ¥2 500 and required that he pay eight months' rent in advance. Sun Peng therefore issued a ¥20 000 check to cover the rent for December through July. Two facts must be recorded about this transaction.

(3) The firm prepaid (paid in advance) the rent for the next eight months in the amount of ¥20 000. As a result, the firm obtained the right to occupy facilities for an eight-

month period. In accounting, this right is considered a form of property.

(4) The firm decreased its cash balance by ¥20 000.

Here is how the firm's financial position looked after this transaction (see Table 2 –2).

Table 2 –2 **Renting Facilities**

	Property			=	Financial Interest
	Cash	+	Prepaid Rent	=	Capital
Previous balances	40 000			=	40 000
(3)		+	20 000		
(4)	–20 000				
New balances	20 000	+	20 000	=	40 000

小提示：

请注意，该笔业务只是引起资产内部项目的增减变化，资产总额仍然保持不变。

2.1.3 Purchasing Equipment for Cash

The manager, Zhang Hua, saw that her first task was to get the business ready for business operations, which were to begin on December 1, 20×8, She bought a computer and other equipment for ¥10 000 and paid for it with a check drawn against the firm's bank account. Two essential elements of this transaction must be recorded.

(5) The firm purchased new property (equipment) for ¥10 000.

(6) The firm paid out ¥10 000 in cash.

Here is the financial position of the business after this transaction was recorded (see Table 2 –3).

Table 2 –3 **Purchasing Equipment**

	Property					=	Financial Interest
	Cash	+	Prepaid Rent	+	Equipment	=	Capital
Previous balances	20 000	+	20 000			=	40 000

Continued

	Property					=	Financial Interest
	Cash	+	Prepaid Rent	+	Equipment	=	Capital
(5)				+	10 000		
(6)	-10 000						
New balances	10 000	+	20 000	+	10 000	=	40 000

Although there was a change in the form of some of the firm's property (cash to equipment), the equation expresses the change that shows the total value of the property remained the same. Sun Peng's financial interest, or equity, was also unchanged. Again, property (Cash, Prepaid Rent, and Equipment) was equal to financial interest (Capital).

小提示:

请注意,需要记入会计系统的活动均为该会计主体的会计事项。业主 Sun Peng 的个人资产,如他的个人银行存款、房子、家具和汽车等财产,与该公司的财产是要分开的。

2.1.4 Purchasing Equipment on Credit

Zhang Hua also bought a copy machine, a fax machine, calculators and other necessary equipment from ABC Corp., at a cost of ¥5 000. ABC Corp., agreed to allow 60 days for the firm to pay the bill. This arrangement is sometimes called buying **on account**. The business has a charge account; or open account, with its suppliers. Amounts that a business must pay in the future under this agreement are known as **accounts payable**. The companies or individuals to whom the amounts are owed are called **creditors**. Analysis of the transaction revealed the following basic elements.

知识点解析:

open account 有两个意思,一是未结清的账户或未结平的账户,二是赊账,即赊购或记账交易,这里是第二个意思。

(7) The firm purchased new property on account from ABC Corp., in the form of equipment that cost ¥5 000.

(8) The firm owed ¥5 000 to ABC Corp.

This increase in equipment was made without an immediate cash payment because ABC Corp. , was willing to accept a claim against Sun Financial Services' property until the bill was paid. There were then two different financial interests or claim against the firm's property—the creditor's claim (Accounts Payable) and the owner's claim (Capital).

Here is how the transaction looked in equation form (see Table 2 -4).

Table 2 -4 Purchasing Equipment on Credit

	Property					=	Financial Interest		
	Cash	+	Prepaid Rent	+	Equipment	=	Accounts Payable	+	Capital
Previous balances	10 000	+	20 000	+	10 000	=		+	40 000
(7)					+5 000				
(8)							+5 000		
New balances	10 000	+	20 000	+	15 000	=	5 000	+	40 000

Test your understanding

The purchase of office supplies on account will ( ).

A. increase an asset and the owner's equity

B. increase one asset and decrease another asset

C. increase an asset and a liability

D. increase an asset and decrease a liability

小提示:

请注意，资产和财务权益可发生同时增加或同时减少的变化，等式两边仍保持平衡。债权人和业主的财务权益即为对该会计主体资产的求偿权。

2.1.5 Purchasing Supplies

From her previous work experience, Zhang Hua was able to estimate the amount of supplies that Sun Financial Services would need to start operations. She placed an order for paper, pens, pencils, folders and other supplies that had a total cost of ¥1 000. The company that sold the items, *Reliable Supplies*, *Inc.* , requires cash payments from businesses that are under six months old. Sun Financial Services therefore included a check with its order. After analyzing the transaction, the major elements listed below were identified.

知识点解析：

supplies 辅料，物料，指零星用品，即次要的，价值较低的材料、工具。这里指办公用品，例如笔、纸、文件夹等。

(9) The firm purchased supplies that cost ￥1 000.

(10) The firm paid ￥1 000 in cash.

Here is how this transaction affected the business's property and financial interests (see Table 2 –5).

Table 2 –5 **Purchasing Supplies**

	Property							=	Financial Interest		
	Cash	+	Supplies	+	Prepaid Rent	+	Equipment	=	Accounts Payable	+	Capital
Previous balances	10 000			+	20 000	+	15 000	=	5 000	+	40 000
(9)		+	1 000								
(10)	–1 000										
New balances	9 000	+	1 000	+	20 000	+	15 000	=	5 000	+	40 000

2.1.6 Paying a Creditor

Zhang Hua decided to pay ￥1 000 to ABC Corp. , to reduce the firm's debt to that business. The analysis of this transaction follows.

(11) The firm paid ￥1 000 in cash.

(12) The claim of ABC Corp. , against the firm decreased by ￥1 000.

The effect of this transaction on the firm's property and financial interests can be expressed in equation form as shown below (see Table 2 –6).

Table 2 –6 **Paying a Creditor**

	Property							=	Financial Interest		
	Cash	+	Supplies	+	Prepaid Rent	+	Equipment	=	Accounts Payable	+	Capital
Previous balances	9 000	+	1 000	+	20 000	+	15 000	=	5 000		40 000
(11)	–1 000										
(12)									–1 000		
New balances	8 000	+	1 000	+	20 000	+	15 000	=	4 000	+	40 000

2.2 Assets, Liabilities and Owner's Equity 资产、负债和所有者权益

Accountants use special accounting terms when they refer to property and financial interests. For example, they refer to property that a business owns as the business's **assets** and to the debts or obligations of the business as its **liabilities**. The owner's financial interest is called **owner's equity**; sometimes it is called net worth. Owner's equity is the preferred term and is the term used throughout this book. At regular intervals Sun Peng will review the status of the firm's assets, liabilities, and owner's equity in a formal report called a **balance sheet**, which is prepared to show the firm's financial position on a given date. Table 2 – 7 shows how the firm's balance sheet looked on November 30, 20 ×8—the day before operations actually began.

知识点解析：

balance sheet 资产负债表，是反映会计主体特定日期财务状况的报表，体现"资产 = 负债 + 所有者权益"的平衡关系，是主要的会计报表之一。资产负债表的格式主要有账户式和报告式，这两种格式仅仅是报告形式的不同，它们所反映的内容都是相同的。

Table 2 – 7 Balance Sheet for Sun Financial Services

SUN FINANCIAL SERVICES

Balance Sheet

November 30, 20 ×8

Assets		Liabilities	
Cash	8 000	Accounts Payable	4 000
Supplies	1 000		
Prepaid Rent	20 000	Owner's Equity	
Equipment	15 000	Capital	40 000
Total Assets	44 000	Total Liabilities and Owner's Equity	44 000

The assets are listed on the left side of the balance sheet and the liabilities and owner's equity on the right side. This arrangement is similar to the equation *property equals financial interest* illustrated earlier. Property was shown on the left side of the equation, and financial interest appeared on the right side.

The balance sheet in Table 2 – 7 shows the amount and types of property the business owned, the amount owed to creditors, and the amount of the owner's interest in the firm on November 30, 20×8. This statement therefore gives Sun Peng a complete picture of the financial position of his business on a specific date.

Test your understanding

Which of the following is not an essential characteristic of a liability?

A. It has arisen as a result of a past transaction or event

B. It represents an internal claim on the entity's assets

C. It represents a present obligation to another entity

D. It requires the transfer of an economic resource to another entity

2.3 The Fundamental Accounting Equation 基本会计等式

The word *balance* in the title "Balance Sheet" has a very special meaning. It serves to emphasize that the total of the figures on the left side of the report must equal, or balance, the total of the figures on the right side. In accounting terms the firm's assets are equal to the total of its liabilities and owner's equity. This equality can be expressed in equation form, as illustrated below. The figures shown are for Sun Financial Services on November 30, 20×8.

Assets	=	Liabilities	+	Owner's Equity
¥44 000	=	¥4 000	+	¥40 000

The relationship between assets and liabilities plus owner's equity is called the **fundamental accounting equation**. The entire accounting process of analyzing, recording, and reporting business transactions is based on the fundamental accounting equation.

知识点解析：

fundamental accounting equation 基本会计等式，又称会计恒等式，即资产＝负债＋所有者权益。该等式的左边说明的是资金的自然属性，即资金的存在形态；该等式的右边说明的是资金的社会属性，即资金的来源渠道。该等式既是资金平衡的理论依据，也是复式记账、设置账户以及编制资产负债表的理论基础。

As with other mathematical equations, if any two parts of the equation are known, the third part can easily be determined. For example, consider the basic accounting equation for Sun Financial Services on November 30, 20 ×8, with some items of information missing.

	Assets	=	Liabilities	+	Owner's Equity
(1)	?	=	¥4 000	+	¥40 000
(2)	¥44 000	=	?	+	¥40 000
(3)	¥44 000	=	¥4 000	+	?

In the first case we can solve for assets by adding liabilities (¥4 000) and owner's equity (¥40 000) to determine that assets are ¥44 000. In the second case we can solve for liabilities by subtracting owner's equity (¥40 000) from assets (¥44 000) to determine that liabilities are ¥4 000. In the third case we can solve for owner's equity by subtracting liabilities (¥4 000) from assets (¥44 000) to determine that owner's equity is ¥40 000.

Test your understanding

Which is the term used to describe the difference between a company's assets and its liabilities, also referred to as the residual interest in the assets of an entity that remains after deducting its liabilities?

A. net profit

B. shares

C. owner's equity

D. revenue

2.3.1 Effects of Revenue and Expenses

Shortly after Sun Financial Services opened for business on December 1, 20 ×8, some of the tenants in the office complex where the business is located became Sun Peng's first clients. Sun Peng also used his contacts in the community to gain other clients. Services to clients began a stream of revenue for the business. **Revenue**, or *income*, is the inflow of money or other assets (including claim to money, such as sales made on credit) that results from sales of goods or services or from the use of money or property.

An **expense**, on the other hand, involves the outflow of money, the use of other assets, or the incurring of a liability. Expense include the costs of any materials, labor, supplies, and services used in an effort to produce revenue. If there is an excess of revenue over expense, the excess represent a **profit**. Making a profit is the reason that people like Sun Peng risk their money by investing it in a business. A firm's accounting records show not only increases and decreases in assets, liabilities and owner's equity but the detailed results of all transactions involving revenue and expenses.

Test your understanding

Which one of the following statements best defines an expense?

A. An expense is any outflow of economic benefits in an accounting period

B. An expense is an outflow of economic benefits resulting from the purchase of resources in an accounting period

C. An expense is an outflow of economic benefits resulting from a claim by a third party

D. An expense is an outflow of economic benefits in an accounting period as a result of the using up of resources or a fall in the value of an asset

Selling Services for Cash

During the month of December 20×8, Sun Financial Services earned a total of ¥10 500 in revenue from clients who paid cash for accounting and bookkeeping services. The receipt of this revenue is analyzed below.

(13) The firm received ¥10 500 in cash for services provided to clients.

(14) The owner's equity increased by ¥10 500 because of this inflow of assets from revenue (Revenue, such as fees earned, always increases the owner's equity).

The revenue figures are usually kept separate from the owner's equity figure until the financial statements are prepared. The revenue should appear in equation form as follows (see Table 2-8).

Table 2-8 **Selling Service for Cash**

			Assets					=	Liabilities	+	Owner's Equity		
	Cash	+	Supp.	+	Prepaid Rent	+	Equip.	=	Accounts Payable	+	Capital	+	Revenue
Previous balances	8 000	+	1 000	+	20 000	+	15 000	=	4 000	+	40 000		
(13)	+10 500												
(14)												+	10 500
New balances	18 500	+	1 000	+	20 000	+	15 000	=	4 000	+	40 000	+	10 500

小提示：

请注意，尽管收入会增加所有者权益，但还是要先单独反映收入，而非直接将其记入所有者权益，这样有助于计算收入总额。

Selling Services on Credit

In December 20×8 Sun Financial Services earned ¥3 500 of revenue from charge account clients. These clients are allowed 30 days to pay. Amounts owed by such customers are known as **accounts receivable**. These accounts represent a new form of asset for the firm—claims for future collection from customers. The analysis of this transaction follows.

(15) The firm acquired a new asset, accounts receivable, of ¥3 500.

(16) The owner's equity was increased by the revenue of ¥3 500. The amount is recorded as revenue because the owner has made a sale and has a claim to an amount to be received in the future.

The following equation shows the effects of this transaction (see Table 2－9).

Table 2－9 **Selling Service on Credit**

	Assets									= Liabilities +		Owner's Equity		
	Cash	+	Accounts Receivable	+	Supp.	+	Prepaid Rent	+	Equip.	=	Accounts Payable	+	Capital	+	Revenue
Previous balances	18 500	+		+	1 000	+	20 000	+	15 000	=	4 000	+	40 000	+	10 500
(15)		+	3 500												
(16)														+	3 500
New balances	18 500	+	3 500	+	1 000	+	20 000	+	15 000	=	4 000	+	40 000	+	14 000

Collecting Receivables

By the end of December 20×8, Sun Financial Services had received ¥1 500 from clients who had previously bought services on account. The firm therefore recognized the following changes.

(17) The firm received ¥1 500 in cash.

(18) Accounts receivable decreased by ¥1 500.

These changes affected the equation as Table 2 – 10.

Table 2 – 10　　Collecting Receivable

	Assets									= Liabilities +		Owner's Equity		
	Cash	+	Accts. Rec.	+	Supp.	+	Prepaid Rent	+	Equip.	= Accounts Payable	+	Capital	+	Revenue
Previous balances	18 500	+	3 500	+	1 000	+	20 000	+	15 000	= 4 000	+	40 000	+	14 000
(17)	+1 500													
(18)			–1 500											
New balances	20 000	+	2 000	+	1 000	+	20 000	+	15 000	= 4 000	+	40 000	+	14 000

小提示：

请注意，从赊账客户收到现金时并不确认收入，该业务只引起资产内部的变化，收入在赊销（sale on credit）时已经确认过了。

2. 3. 2 Paying Expenses

So far Sun Peng has done very well. His equity has increased by sizable revenues. However, keeping a business running costs money, and these expenses reduce owner's equity. The expense figures are kept separate from the figures for the owner's capital and revenue. The separate record of expenses is kept for the same reason as the separate record of revenue is kept—to help analyze operations for the period.

Employee' Salaries

During December 20 ×8, the first month of operations, Sun Financial Services hired an accounting clerk to help in the business. The firm paid ￥2 500 in salaries for this employee. This transaction is analyzed as follows.

(19) Cash was reduced by payment of ￥2 500 to cover the salaries.

(20) The owner's equity decreased by the ￥2 500 outflow of assets for salaries expense.

The effect of the salaries expense is shown as Table 2 – 11.

Table 2 – 11 **Paying Salaries for Employee**

	Assets									=	Liabilities	+	Owner's Equity				
	Cash	+	Accts. Rec.	+	Supp.	+	Prepaid Rent	+	Equip.	=	Accounts Payable	+	Capital	+	Revenue	–	Expenses
Previous balances	20 000	+	2 000	+	1 000	+	20 000	+	15 000	=	4 000	+	40 000	+	14 000		
(19)	–2 500																
(20)																–	2 500
New balances	17 500	+	2 000	+	1 000	+	20 000	+	15 000	=	4 000	+	40 000	+	14 000	–	2 500

Utilities Expense

At the end of December 20 ×8, Sun Financial Services receive a ¥300 bill for the utilities that is had used during the month. A check was issued to pay the bill immediately. This transaction was another business expense and its analysis follows.

(21) Cash was reduce by the payment of ¥300 for utilities.

(22) The owner's equity decrease by ¥300 because of the expense incurred.

The effect of the utilities expense is shown as Table 2 –12.

Table 2 – 12 **Paying Utilities Expense**

	Assets									=	Liabilities	+	Owner's Equity				
	Cash	+	Accts. Rec.	+	Supp.	+	Prepaid Rent	+	Equip.	=	Accounts Payable	+	Capital	+	Revenue	–	Expenses
Previous balances	17 500	+	2 000	+	1 000	+	20 000	+	15 000	=	4 000	+	40 000	+	14 000	–	2 500
(21)	–300																
(22)																–	300
New balances	17 200	+	2 000	+	1 000	+	20 000	+	15 000	=	4 000	+	40 000	+	14 000	–	2 800

2.3.3 Effect of Owner's Withdrawals

On December 30, 20 ×8, Sun Peng withdraw ¥1 000 in cash from the business to pay for personal expenses. **Withdrawals** are funds taken from the business by the owner to pay for personal use. Withdrawals are not a business expense but a decrease of the owner's equity in the business. The separate entity assumption requires the recording of transactions of each entity in separate records.

The effect of Sun Peng's withdrawal of ¥1 000 in cash for personal expenses is shown below.

(23) Cash was reduced by the ¥1 000 withdrawal.

(24) The owner's equity decreased by ¥1 000 because the withdrawn funds decreased the total assets of the firm.

After this transaction was recorded, the equation appeared as Table 2 – 13.

Table 2 – 13　　Effect of Owner's Withdrawals

	Assets									= Liabilities +		Owner's Equity				
	Cash	+	Accts. Rec.	+	Supp.	+	Prepaid Rent	+	Equip.	=	Accounts Payable	+	Capital	+	Revenue	–	Expenses
Previous balances	17 200	+	2 000	+	1 000	+	20 000	+	15 000	=	4 000	+	40 000	+	14 000	–	2 800
(23)	–1 000																
(24)													–1 000				
New balances	16 200	+	2 000	+	1 000	+	20 000	+	15 000	=	4 000	+	39 000	+	14 000	–	2 800

2.4 The Income Statement　利润表

The **income statement** is a formal report of the results of business operations for a specific period of time such as a month, a quarter, or a year. In contrast, the balance sheet reports the financial condition of the business on a given date such as June 30 or December 31. The balance sheet shows what the business owns and owes as well as the amount of the owner's equity in the business. The income statement shows the revenue earned by the business and the expenses of doing business.

知识点解析：

income statement 损益表、利润表。在英国和澳大利亚等国也称作 profit and loss statement。指反映企业的销售收入、销售成本、毛利、其他收益和其他支出等项目，并确定一个期间净利润（亏损）的财务报表，即反映企业一定期间经营成果的报表。

The income statement is sometimes called a profit and loss statement or a statement of income and expenses. The most common term is income statement. The income statement shown in Table 2 – 14, illustrates how Sun Financial Services would present the results of its first month of operation.

Table 2 – 14 Income Statement for Sun Financial Services

SUN FINANCIAL SERVICRS

Income Statement

Month Ended December 31, 20 ×8

Revenue		
Fees Income		14 000
Expenses		
Salaries Expense	2 500	
Utilities Expense	300	
Total Expenses		2 800
Net Income		11 200

小提示：

请注意，利润表的表头表明了谁、什么和何时。第一行是主体的名称（who），第二行是报表的名称（what），第三行是报表的日期（when）。如果是一季度的利润表，则表示为“Three – Month Period Ended March 31, 20 ×8”；如果报告从 1 月 1 日至 12 月 31 日的日历年度的经营成果，则表示为“Year Ended December 31, 20 ×8”；若是结束于 12 月 31 日以外的一年的报告期，则表示为如“Fiscal Year Ended June 30, 20 ×8”或“Fiscal Year Ended November 30, 20 ×8”。

The difference between income from services provided or goods sold and the amount spent to operate the business is reported at the bottom of the income statement. **Net income** results when the revenue for the period is greater than the expenses. when expenses are greater than revenue, the result is a **net loss**. In the rare case when revenue and expenses are equal, the firm is said to **break even**. The income statement in Table 2 – 14 shows a net income because revenue was greater than expenses.

知识点解析：

break even 保本点，又称 break-even point。保本点是指企业处于既不盈利也不亏损状态下的销量，也可以定义为“收入和总成本相等时的销量”。保本点可以用数量表示，也可以用金额表示。总之，保本点就是企业生存的最低销售量，或是企业的最低销售额。

2.5 The Statement of Owner's Equity and The Balance Sheet 所有者权益表和资产负债表

The income statement by itself is meaningful to business owners, managers, and other interested parties. However, it is even more informative when considered in relation to the assets and equities that were involved in earning the revenue. Therefore, the statement of owner's equity and the balance sheet are prepared to give the details of these assets and equities.

The **statements of owner's equity** reports the changes that have occurred in the owner's financial interest during the reporting period. This statement is prepared before the balance sheet so that the amount of the ending capital balance is available for presentation on the balance sheet. The statement of owner's equity for Sun Financial Services is shown in Table 2 – 15.

Table 2 – 15 Statement of Owner's Equity for Sun Financial Services

SUN FINANCIAL SERVICRS

Statement of Owner's Equity

Month Ended December 31, 20×8

Capital, December 1, 20×8		40 000
Net Income for December	11 200	
Less Withdrawals for December	1 000	
Increase in Capital		10 200
Capital, December 31, 20×8		50 200

小提示：

请注意，利润表是在所有者权益表和资产负债表之前编制的。编制所有者权益表是为了反映报告期所有者权益的变动，净利润使所有者权益增加，净亏损使所有者权益减少。编制所有者权益表之后，所有者权益的期末余额将列示在资产负债表中。

In addition to net income and net loss, the statement of owner's equity is also affected by additional investments by the owner. Since Sun Peng did not make any additional investments during the month of December, this item does not appear in the preceding statement of owner's equity.

Test your understanding

Which one of the following represents the expanded accounting equation?

A. Assets = Liabilities + Common stock + Dividends − Revenue − Expenses

B. Assets + Dividends + Expenses = Liabilities + Common stock + Revenue

C. Assets − Liabilities − Dividends = Common stock + Revenue − Expenses

D. Assets = Revenue + Expenses − Liabilities

Additional investments and net income increase owner's equity. Additional investments may be in cash or other assets such as equipment. If an investment is made in a form other than cash, the investment should be recorded at its **fair market value**. Fair market value is the present worth of an asset or the price the asset would bring if sold on the open market. Withdrawals and net losses decrease owner's equity.

知识点解析：

fair market value 公允价值，又称 fair value。国际财务报告准则将公允价值定义为"市场参与者之间在计量日进行的有序交易中出售一项资产所收到的价格或转移一项负债所支付的价格"，有时也被称为"脱手价"。现在的历史成本是过去的公允价值，现在的公允价值即未来的历史成本。

The final totals in the fundamental accounting equation for the asset and liability accounts plus the statement of owner's equity supply the figures that are required for preparing a balance sheet for Sun Financial Services as of December 31, 20×8 (see Table 2－16).

Table 2－16　The Final Totals in the Equation

	Assets									=	Liabilities	+	Owner's Equity				
	Cash	+	Accts. Rec.	+	Supp.	+	Prepaid Rent	+	Equip.	=	Accounts Payable	+	Capital	+	Revenue	−	Expenses
New balances	16 200	+	2 000	+	1 000	+	20 000	+	15 000	=	4 000	+	39 000	+	14 000	−	2 800

The balance sheet in Table 2 – 17 is prepared from the figures in the above equation and from the statement of owner's equity. The balance sheet shows the types and amounts of property that the business owns (asset), the amounts owed to creditors (liabilities), and the amount of the owner's equity on the reporting date.

Table 2 – 17　　Balance Sheet of Sun Financial Services

SUN FINANCIAL SERVICRS

Balance Sheet

November 30, 20 ×8

Assets		Liabilities	
Cash	16 200	Accounts Payable	4 000
Accounts Receivable	2 000		
Supplies	1 000		
Prepaid Rent	20 000	Owner's Equity	
Equipment	15 000	Capital	50 200
Total Assets	54 200	Total Liabilities and Owner's Equity	54 200

In preparing a balance sheet, keep in mind the following details:

(1) The three-line heading of the balance sheet gives the firm's name (who), the title of the report (what), and the date of the report (when). Every balance sheet heading contains these three lines.

(2) On this form of balance sheet, the account form, the total of the assets always appears on the same horizontal line as the total of the liabilities and owner's equity.

本章小结：

会计工作程序始于对经济业务或会计事项的分析。会计师要分析每一笔经济业务，以确定其对会计恒等式的影响，即资产 = 负债 + 所有者权益。

资产负债表账户与利润表账户是相关联的。所有者权益的变化是由收入和费用引起的，收入和费用反映在利润表上，它们之间的差额就是企业当期的净利润或净损失。当期的净利润和所有者的投资增加所有者权益，当期净损失和所有者的个人提款会使所有者权益减少。

资产负债表是反映企业某一特定日期的资产、负债和所有者权益三要素财务状况的会计报表，并且体现基本会计等式的平衡关系。由于期末所有者权益的金额要呈报在资产负债表上，因此资产负债表应在所有者权益表之后编制。

Self – Review & Questions 自测题

1. What is a business transaction?

2. What is the difference between buying for cash and buying on account?

3. Describe a transaction that increase an asset and owner's equity.

4. Describe a transaction that will cause Accounts Payable and Cash to decrease by ¥400.

5. What are withdrawals and how do they affect the basic accounting equation?

6. If an owner gives personal tools to the business, how is the transaction recorded?

7. Which financial statement is prepared first? Why?

8. If one side of the fundamental accounting equation is decreased, what will happen to the other side? Why?

9. What items are included in the headings of financial statements?

Translations 翻译题

Translate the following English into Chinese or Chinese into English.

1. Accurate and informative financial records and statements are necessary so that business people can make sound decisions.

2. Accounting information helps to determine whether a profit has been made, the amount of the assets on hand, the amount owed to creditors, and the amount of owner's equity.

3. Any well-run and efficiently managed business will have a good accounting system to provide timely and useful information.

4. The difference between revenue and expenses is the net income or net loss of the business for the period.

5. Withdrawals are funds taken from the business to pay for personal expenses. Withdrawals are not business expenses but they decrease the owner's equity in the business.

6. 资产是指企业所拥有或控制的、能够在未来给企业带来利益的资源。

7. 负债是企业过去的交易、事项形成的现时业务，履行该义务预期会导致经济利益流出企业。

8. 会计通常被称作商业语言，企业只有建立了一个完善的会计信息系统，才能提供完整、及时的财务信息以帮助人们做出更优的决策。

Exercises 练习题

Exercise 2 -1

Just before Chen Medical Supply opened for business, Chen Jie, the owner, had the following assets and liabilities. Determine the amounts that would appear in the firm's fundamental accounting equation (Assets = Liabilities + Owner's Equity).

Cash	8 950
Laboratory Equipment	21 250
Laboratory Supplies	1 200
Loan Payable	3 400
Accounts Payable	2 050

Exercise 2 -2

The financial data shown below is for the dental practice of Dr. Wang when she began operations on June 1, 20×8. Determine the amounts that would appear in Dr. Wang's balance sheet.

1. Owes ¥15 000 to a equipment company.
2. Has cash balance of ¥5 650.
3. Has dental supplies of ¥2 340.
4. Owes ¥2 800 to a furniture company.
5. Has dental equipment of ¥23 700.
6. Has office furniture of ¥3 450.

Exercise 2 -3

Indicate the impact of each of the transactions below on the fundamental accounting equation (Assets = Liabilities + Owner's equity) by placing a " + " to indicate an increase, and a " − " to indicate a decrease. The first translation is entered as an example.

	Assets	=	Liabilities	+	Owner's equation
Transaction 1	+				+

Transactions:

1. Owner invested ¥10 000 in the business.
2. Purchased ¥1 000 supplies on account.
3. Purchased equipment for ¥5 000 cash.
4. Paid ¥700 for rent.
5. Performed service for ¥1 200 cash.
6. Paid ¥200 for utilities.
7. Performed services for ¥1 500 on account.
8. Received ¥750 from charge customers.
9. Paid salaries of ¥1 200 to employees.
10. Paid ¥500 to a creditor on account.

Exercise 2 – 4

A publishing company had the transactions listed below during the month of April 20×8. Show how each transaction would be recorded in the accounting equation. Compute the totals at the end of the month. The headings to be used in the equation follow.

Assets					=	Liabilities	+	Owner's Equity				
Cash	+	Accounts Receivable	+	Equipment	=	Accounts Payable	+	Capital	+	Revenue	−	Expenses

Transactions:

1. Zhao Yong started the business with a cash investment of ¥18 000.
2. Purchased equipment for ¥7 000 on credit.
3. Performed services for ¥900 in cash.
4. Purchased additional equipment for ¥1 500 in cash.
5. Performed services for ¥2 100 on credit.
6. Paid salaries of ¥1 600 to employees.
7. Received ¥700 cash from charge account customers.
8. Paid ¥3 500 to a creditor on account.

Exercise 2 – 5

The Office Supply Service Center had the following revenue and expenses during the month ended June 30, 20×8. Did the firm earn a net income or incur a net loss for the period? What was the amount?

Fees for computer repairs	8 200
Rent Expenses	900
Salaries Expenses	4 275
Telephone Expenses	180
Fees for typewriter repairs	1 260
Utilities Expenses	375

Exercise 2 -6

On December 1, 20 ×8, Li Ming opened an engineering firm. During December his firm had the following transactions involving revenue and expenses. Did the firm earn a net income or incur a net loss for the period? What was the amount?

1. Paid ¥800 for rent.
2. Provided services for ¥1 050 in cash.
3. Paid ¥150 for telephone service.
4. Paid salaries of ¥1 900 to employees.
5. Provided services for ¥1 300 on credit.
6. Paid ¥100 for office cleaning service.

Exercise 2 -7

At the beginning of September 20 ×8, Zhang Qiang started a firm that offers advice about investing and managing money. On September 30, 20 ×8, the accounting records of the business showed the following information. Prepare an income statement and a statement of owner's equity for the month of September 20 ×8. Prepare a balance sheet as of September 30, 20 ×8.

Cash	7 600
Accounts Receivable	600
Office Supplies	400
Office Equipment	8 550
Accounts Payable	700
Capital, September 1, 20 ×8	5 400
Fees Income	16 700
Rent Expense	1 050
Salaries Expense	3 400
Telephone Expense	200
Withdrawals	1 000

Supplementary Reading 扩展阅读

Internal Control

Internal control is defined as a process that is designed by management in order to provide reasonable assurance that the organization's objectives are being met. The objectives relevant to internal controls include: (1) improving the effectiveness of management decision making and the efficiency of business processes, (2) increasing the reliability of accounting information, and (3) fostering compliance with rules and regulations. There are five elements in internal control.

1. Control Environment

Control environment refers to the organization's overall approach and attitude towards designing and implementing policies and procedures that foster achievement of financial reporting objectives. The most important aspects of the control environment are management's attitudes and incentive factors providing an indication of the effectiveness of the control environment including clear lines of authority, responsibility and performance evaluation, the existence of a competent, independent internal audit department, clearly stated and documented personnel policies, an active audit committee consisting of independent members of the board of directors, outside influences, and constraints imposed on the organization.

2. Risk Assessment

Risk assessment refers that management should put in place a set of procedures whose purpose is to identify, analyze and manage the risks related to accurate financial reporting. Circumstances creating significant risks include changes in environment, changes in personnel, changes in information systems, rate of growth, existence of new technologies, changes in product lines or lines of business, corporate restructuring or merger activity, and accounting changes.

3. Control Activities

Control activities are the specific policies and procedures designed and implemented by management to minimize the risks associated with the control objectives.

Physical controls limit the access to assets and records. Some duties need to be segregated, and they include the following situations: (1) the custody of assets, the recording of transactions and the authorization of transactions should be performed by different individuals; (2) the general guidelines related to the segregation of duties, including segregating asset custody from the accounting function, segregating transaction authorization from asset custody, segregating operating functions from accounting functions, and segregating within the accounting and data processing function.

4. Communication

Communication means the management need to communicate the transaction information to the public.

5. Monitoring

Monitoring activities are designed to provide information to management about potential and actual breakdowns in the control system that could allow the information system to produce unreliable information reporting.

CHAPTER 3 Using T Accounts
T 型账户的运用

本章学习目标

1. 掌握如何建立资产、负债、所有者权益、收入和费用的 T 型账户。
2. 根据对业务交易的分析，能够将资金的增减变化记入恰当的 T 型账户。
3. 掌握如何确定一个账户的余额。
4. 学会编制试算平衡表。
5. 编制利润表、所有者权益表和资产负债表，并理解三者之间的勾稽关系。

本章核心术语

account balance 账户余额
accounts 账户
chart of accounts 会计科目表
credit 贷记，贷方
debit 借记，借方
double-entry system 复式记账法
Drawing account 提款账户
permanent account 永久性账户
T account T 型账户
temporary account 临时性账户
trial balance 试算平衡表

The accounting equation is used to analyze a firm's transactions and determine their effects on the firm's assets, liabilities, and owner's equity. The firm's financial position is reported on the balance sheet and the results of its operations for a period of time are reported on the income statement. How to keep records of the changes that are caused by business transaction? These records are an essential part of all accounting systems.

3.1 Accounts for Assets, Liabilities and Owner's Equity 资产、负债和所有者权益账户

The accounting equation is a tool for analyzing the effects of business transactions. It would be awkward, though, to record every transaction in the equation format if a business had many transactions. Instead, separate written records called **accounts** are kept for the business's assets, liabilities and owner's equity. Accounts are kept so that financial information can be analyzed, recorded, classified, summarized and reported. Accounts are identified by their account **classification**; that is, as asset accounts (the property a business owns), liability accounts (the debts of the business), or owner's equity accounts (the owner's financial interest in the business). The title of each account describes the type of property, the debt, or the financial interest.

One type of account that accountants use to analyze transactions is a **T account**. This account consists of two lines, one vertical and one horizontal, that resemble the letter **T**. The title of the account is written on the horizontal (top) line. Increases and decreases in the account are entered on different sides of the vertical line.

T accounts for assets, liabilities and owner's equity follow.

Assets		Liabilities		Owner's Equity	
+	−	−	+	−	+
Record increase	Record decrease	Record decrease	Record increase	Record decrease	Record increase

3.1.1 Recording a Cash Investment

Asset accounts record the items of value owned by a business. The location of items in the fundamental accounting equation determines where amounts are recorded in the T accounts. For instance, when Sun Peng invested ¥40 000 in the business, the office manager for Sun Financial Services, Zhang Hua, set up a separate account for the asset cash. The cash investment of ¥40 000 (1) is entered on the left side of the account because assets always appear on the left side of the accounting equation. The plus and minus signs shown below in the T account do not normally appear in the accounts. However, they are presented here to help you identify increases (+) and decreases (−) in accounts.

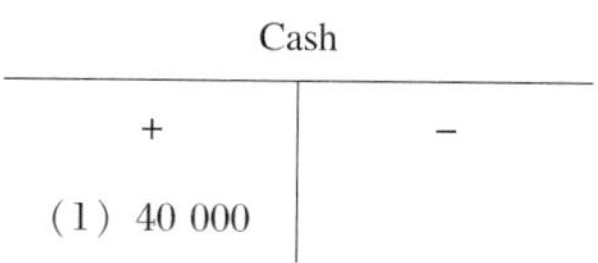

Since increases are recorded on the left side of asset accounts, decreases are recorded on the right side.

Owner's equity accounts show the financial interest of the owner of the business. The account called Capital, is used to record Sun Peng's ¥40 000 investment. Because owner's equity always appears on the right side of the accounting equation, Zhang Hua entered the opening balance of ¥40 000 (2) on the right side of the Capital account.

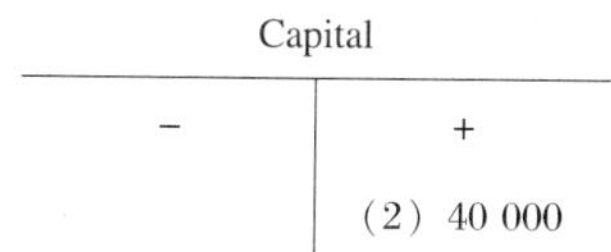

Since the right side of the owner's equity account is used to record increases in owner's equity, the left side must be used to record decreases.

3.1.2 Recording Prepaid Rent

When Sun Financial Services rented its facilities, the lease specified that eight months' rent must be paid in advance. Sun Peng issued a check for ¥20 000 to make the necessary payment. As a result, the firm obtained the right to occupy the facilities for an eight-month period. This right is accounted for as property—an asset. Thus the transaction is analyzed as follows.

(3) The firm acquired an asset, totaling ¥20 000, in the form of prepaid rent.
(4) The firm paid ¥20 000 in cash.

To record the prepaid rent (3), a new asset account called Prepaid Rent is opened; the ¥20 000 is entered on the left, or increase, side of the Prepaid Rent account.

Prepaid Rent

+	−
(3) 20 000	

Since the cash payment (4) reduced the firm's cash balance, the ¥20 000 is recorded on the right, or decrease, side of the Cash account.

Cash	
+	−
(1) 40 000	(4) 20 000

3.1.3 Recording a Cash Purchase of Equipment

When Sun Financial Services purchased equipment for ¥10 000 in cash, the transaction was analyzed as follows.

(5) The firm purchased new assets in the form of equipment at a cost of ¥10 000.

(6) The firm paid ¥10 000 in cash.

To record the purchase of equipment (5), a new asset account for equipment was opened and ¥10 000 was entered on the left, or increase, side.

Equipment	
+	−
(5) 10 000	

The payment of ¥10 000 in cash (6) is entered on the right side of the Cash account because decreases in assets are recorded on the right side.

Cash	
+	−
(1) 40 000	(4) 20 000
	(6) 10 000

3.1.4 Recording a Credit Purchase of Equipment

Liabilities are amounts owed by a business to its creditors. Like owner's equity, liabilities always appear on the right side of the accounting equation. Thus increases are recorded on the right side of liability accounts, and decreases are recorded on the left side.

When Sun Financial Services bought a copy machine, a fax machine, calculators, and other necessary equipment for ¥5 000 on credit from ABC Corp. , the transaction was analyzed as follows.

(7) The firm purchased new assets in the form of equipment at a cost of ¥5 000.

(8) The firm owed ¥5 000 as an account payable to ABC Corp.

The ¥5 000 increase in equipment (7) is entered on the left side of the Equipment account.

Equipment

+	−
(5) 10 000	
(7) 5 000	

A new account is opened for the liability Accounts Payable to record the amount owed to ABC Corp. (8). The ¥5 000 is entered on the right, or increase, side of this account because liabilities appear on the right side of the accounting equation.

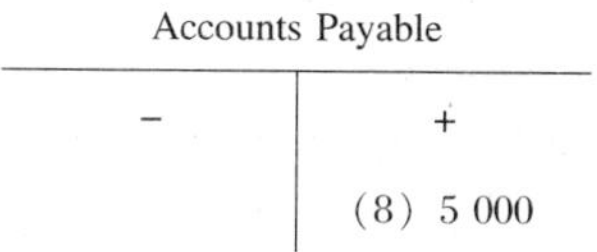

Accounts Payable

−	+
	(8) 5 000

3.1.5 Recording a Cash Purchase of Supplies

When Sun Financial Services purchased supplies for ¥1 000 in cash, the transaction was analyzed as follows.

(9) The firm purchased new assets in the form of supplies at a cost of ¥1 000.

(10) The firm paid ¥1 000 in cash.

To record the purchase of supplies (9), a new asset account for supplies was opened and ¥1 000 was entered on the left, or increase, side.

Supplies	
+	−
(9) 1 000	

The payment of ¥1 000 in cash (10) is entered on the right side of the Cash account because decreases in assets are recorded on the right side of asset accounts.

Cash	
+	−
(1) 40 000	(4) 20 000
	(6) 10 000
	(10) 1 000

3.1.6 Recording Payment to a Creditor

On November 30, 20×8, the business paid ¥1 000 to ABC Corp., to apply against the debt of ¥5 000 shown in Accounts Payable. The analysis of this transaction follows.

(11) The firm paid ¥1 000 in cash.

(12) The claim of ABC Corp., against the firm was reduced by ¥1 000.

The decrease in cash (11) is entered on the right (decrease) side of the Cash account. The decrease in the liability (12) is entered on the left (decrease) side of the Accounts Payable account.

Cash	
+	−
(1) 40 000	(4) 20 000
	(6) 10 000
	(10) 1 000
	(11) 1 000

Accounts Payable	
−	+
(12) 1 000	(8) 5 000

The balance of an account is normally recorded on the increase side of the account. The increase side of the account is the **normal balance** of the account. As previously discussed, the increase side of an account depends upon whether the account is classified as an asset, liability, or owner's equity account. A summary of the procedures to increase or decrease accounts and normal balance of accounts in the basic accounting equation follows.

Assets	
+	−
Increase (Normal Bal.)	Decrease

Liabilities	
−	+
Decrease	Increase (Normal Bal.)

Owner's Equity	
−	+
Decrease	Increase (Normal Bal.)

A summary of the account balances for Sun Financial Services is shown in Table 3 – 1. The firm's position after these transactions can be given in equation form.

Table 3 – 1　　T – Account Balances for Sun Financial Services

Cash	
+	−
(1) 40 000	(4) 20 000
	(6) 10 000
	(10) 1 000
	(11) 1 000
Bal. 8 000	

Accounts Payable	
−	+
(12) 1 000	(8) 5 000
	Bal. 4 000

Capital	
−	+
	(1) 40 000
	Bal. 4 000

Supplies	
+	−
(9) 1 000	
Bal. 1 000	

Prepaid Rent	
+	−
(3) 20 000	
Bal. 20 000	

Equipment	
+	−
(5) 10 000	
(7) 5 000	
Bal. 15 000	

A formal balance sheet prepared for November 30, 20×8, is shown in Table 3-2.

Table 3-2 **Balance Sheet for Sun Financial Services**

SUN FINANCIAL SERVICRS

Balance Sheet

November 30, 20×8

Assets		Liabilities	
Cash	8 000	Accounts Payable	4 000
Supplies	1 000		
Prepaid Rent	20 000	Owner's Equity	
Equipment	15 000	Capital	40 000
Total Assets	44 000	Total Liabilities and Owner's Equity	44 000

3.2 Accounts for Revenue and Expenses 收入和费用账户

Some owner's equity accounts can be further classified as revenue or expense accounts. Many business transactions involve revenue and expenses. Separate accounts are used to record these amounts. Let's examine the revenue and expense transactions of Sun Financial Services for December to see how they are recorded.

3.2.1 Recording Revenue from Services Sold for Cash

During December the business earned a total of ¥10 500 in revenue from clients who paid cash for bookkeeping and accounting services. The office manager made the following analysis.

(13) The firm received ¥10 500 in cash.

(14) The owner's equity increased by ¥10 500 because of this inflow of assets from revenue.

Zhang Hua recorded the receipt of cash (13) by entering ¥10 500 on the left (increase) side of the asset account Cash.

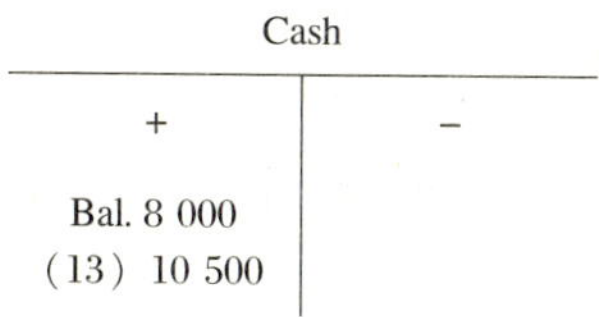

How is the increase in owner's equity recorded? One way would be to record the ¥10 500 on the right side of the Capital account. However, the preferred way is to keep the revenue figures separate from the owner's investment until the end of the month or until financial reports are prepared. Therefore, Zhang Hua opens a new account called Fees Income (a revenue account). Remember that revenue is a subdivision of owner's equity. At this point in its operations, Sun Financial Services needs just one revenue account. which is called Fees Income. The title of this account describes the specific type of revenue recorded in it.

The ¥10 500 of revenue (14) is entered on the right side of the Fees Income account because revenue increases owner's equity and an owner's equity account is increased on the right side.

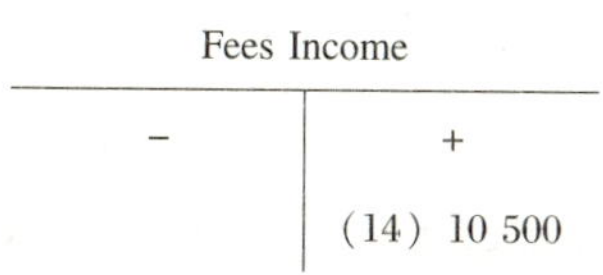

Since the right side of the revenue account is used to record increases, the left side is used to record decreases. Decreases in a revenue account may be required by corrections, by transfers to other accounts, or by refunds. However, such entries are not required often.

Different accounts are used for different types of revenue. For instance, in a business where goods are sold, an accountant would set up a revenue account called Sales. When more than one revenue account is used, the accounts are classified under the heading *Revenue* on the income statement, and the total of their balances would be the total operating revenue of the business for the accounting period.

3.2.2 Recording Revenue from Services Sold on Credit

During December Sun Financial Services also earned revenue of ¥3 500 from charge account clients. The office manager's analysis showed the following effects.

(15) The firm obtained a new asset—accounts receivable of ¥3 500.

(16) The owner's equity was increased by ¥3 500 of revenue.

To record this transaction, Zhang Hua first opened a new asset account called Accounts Receivable and entered the ¥3 500 (15) on the left (increase) side of the account. Zhang Hua entered the ¥3 500 increase in owner's equity (16) on the right (increase) side of the Fees Income account.

Accounts Receivable	
+	−
(15) 3 500	

Fees Income	
−	+
	(14) 10 500
	(16) 3 500

3. 2. 3 Recording Collections from Accounts Receivable

When charge account clients paid a total of ¥1 500 to apply to their accounts, Zhang Hua made the following analysis.

(17) The firm received ¥1 500 in cash.

(18) Accounts receivable decreased by ¥1 500.

Recording this information involved the use of two asset accounts. Zhang Hua entered the ¥1 500 increase in cash (17) on the left side of the Cash account and the ¥1 500 decrease in accounts receivable (18) on the right side of the Accounts Receivable account.

Cash	
+	−
Bal. 8 000	
(13) 10 500	
(17) 1 500	

Accounts Receivable	
+	−
(15) 3 500	(18) 1 500

3. 2. 4 Recording an Expense for Salaries

Like other firms, Sun Financial Services had expenses in running its business. The first expense was for employees' salaries of ¥2 500. The office manager determined that this expense had the following effects.

(19) The payment of ¥2 500 for salaries reduced the asset Cash.

(20) Expenses increased by ¥2 500, specifically the Salaries Expense account.

The decrease in cash (19) is recorded on the right (decrease) side of the asset account Cash.

Cash

+	−
Bal. 8 000	(19) 2 500
(13) 10 500	
(17) 1 500	

The decrease in owner's equity that results from the expense could be entered on the left (decrease) side of the Capital account. However, the preferred way is to keep expenses separate from the owner's equity account until the end of the month, or until financial reports are prepared. Like revenue, expenses are a subdivision of owner's equity. This subdivision is used to classify and summarize the various costs of operating the business.

A new account called Salaries Expense is opened for Sun Financial Services. The account title describes the specific type of expense recorded in the account.

The ¥2 500 for salaries (20) is entered on the left side of the Salaries Expense account because decrease owner's equity and an owner's equity account is decreased on the left side. Remember that an increase in an expense brings about a decrease in owner's equity. The plus and minus signs shown in the illustration below indicate the effect on the expense account, not the effect on owner's equity.

Salaries Expense

+	−
(20) 2 500	

Other kinds of expense will be recorded in separate accounts, each with its own descriptive title. For example, the payment of monthly utility bills will be recorded in an account called Utilities Expense. Salaries Expense and Utilities Expense are classified under the heading *Expenses* on the income statement. The total of all such account balances is the total operating expenses of the business for the accounting period.

3.2.5 Recording an Expense for Utilities

During December 20×8 Sun Financial Services also had an expense of ¥300 for utilities, which it paid by issuing a check. Zhang Hua made the following analysis of this transaction.

(21) The payment of ¥300 for utilities reduce the asset Cash.

(22) The account Utilities Expense was increased by ¥300.

The reduction in cash (21) was recorded by an entry on the right (decrease) side of the asset account Cash.

Cash

+	−
Bal. 8 000	(19) 2 500
(13) 10 500	(21) 300
(17) 1 500	

To record the expense (22), the ¥300 is entered on the left (increase) side of the Utilities Expense account.

Utilities Expense

+	−
(22) 300	

Increase in expenses are recorded on the left side of expense accounts because expenses reduce owner's equity. Decrease in expenses are recorded on the right side of the accounts. Decrease in expenses may result from corrections, transfers to other accounts, or refunds. However, such entries are not required often.

3.3 The Drawing Account 提款账户

In sole proprietorships and partnerships, the owners generally do not pay themselves salaries. To obtain funds for personal living expenses, owners make withdrawals of cash against previously earned profits that have become part of their capital or against profits that are expected in the future. A special type of owner's equity account called a **drawing account** is set up to record these withdrawals.

知识点解析：

drawing account 提款账户。这是用于独资企业和合伙企业的一个过渡性账户，记录独资企业主或合伙人从企业中提取用于个人消费的现金或其他资产。该账户的余额期末要结转到业主或合伙人的资本账户，是资本的抵减项目。

Since withdrawals of cash decrease owner's equity, withdrawals can be recorded on the left side of the Capital account. However, the preferred way is to separate withdrawals from the owner's equity account until the end of the month. On December 30, 20×8, Sun Peng withdrew ¥1 000 in cash from the business to pay for personal expenses. The effect of the withdrawal is shown below.

(23) Cash was reduced by the ¥1 000 withdrawal.

(24) The amount of cash the owner withdrew from the business increased by ¥1 000.

The decrease in cash (23) is recorded with an entry on the right (decrease) side of the asset account Cash.

Cash

+	−
Bal. 8 000	(19) 2 500
(13) 10 500	(21) 300
(17) 1 500	(23) 1 000

To record the increase in withdrawals (24), the ¥1 000 is entered on the left (increase) side of the Drawing account. The balance of the drawing account decrease the capital account and is reported on the statement of owner's equity as withdrawals for the period.

Drawing

+	−
(24) 1 000	

A Summary of the relationship between the capital account and the revenue, expense and drawing accounts is shown in Table 3-3.

Table 3 – 3 **The Relationship between Owner's Equity and Revenue, Expenses, and Withdrawals**

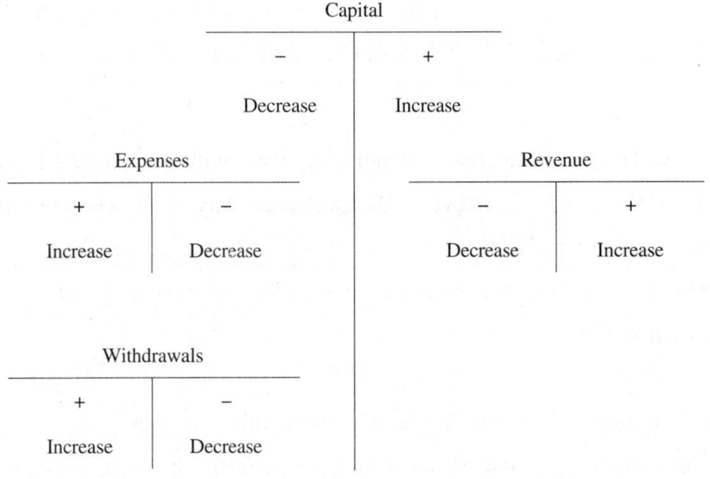

3.4 The Rules of Debit and Credit 复式记账法则

Accountants do not say "left side" or "right side" when they talk about making entries in accounts. They use the term **debit** when they refer to an entry on the left side of an account and the term **credit** when they refer to an entry on the right side of an account. For example, accountants increase assets by debiting asset accounts, and they decrease assets by crediting asset accounts. However, accountants increase liabilities by crediting liability accounts and decrease liabilities by debiting liability accounts. Table 3 – 4 summarizes the rules for debiting and crediting accounts.

Table 3 – 4 **Rules for Debits and Credits**

Assets Accounts		Liabilities Accounts		Owner's Capital Account	
Debit	Credit	Debit	Credit	Debit	Credit
+	–	–	+	–	+
Increase Side (Normal Bal.)	Decrease Side	Decrease Side	Increase Side (Normal Bal.)	Decrease Side	Increase Side (Normal Bal.)

Continued

Owner's Drawing Account		Revenue Accounts		Expense Accounts	
Debit	Credit	Debit	Credit	Debit	Credit
+	−	−	+	+	−
Increase Side (Normal Bal.)	Decrease Side	Decrease Side	Increase Side (Normal Bal.)	Increase Side (Normal Bal.)	Decrease Side

知识点解析：

debit 借记、借方，credit 贷记、贷方，是借贷记账法的记账符号。最初运用"借"和"贷"是为了记录借贷资本家的货币的存入与放出，即把从债权人那里收到的存款记在"贷主"名下，表示自身的债务；将支付给债务人的放款记在"借主"名下，表示自身的债权。后来随着经济活动的日益复杂，借、贷两字就逐渐失去了原来的含义，转化为纯粹的记账符号，表示资金增减变化的方向。

The analysis of each transaction produces at least two effects. The effect of an entry on the debit, or left, side of one account is balanced by the effect of an entry on the credit, or right, side of another account. For this reason, the modern system of accounting is usually called the **double-entry system**. This system involves recording both effects of every transaction to present a complete picture. The balancing relationship also explains why both sides of the equations shown in Chapter 1 are always equal.

知识点解析：

double-entry system 复式记账法，又称 double entry bookkeeping 复式簿记，最常见的复式簿记是"借贷记账法"。"借贷记账法"以"借""贷"为记账符号，以"有借必有贷，借贷必相等"为记账原则，即以相等的金额在两个或两个以上的账户反映每一项经济业务。公元1300年，意大利北部城市首先使用复式记账法，1494年，卢卡·帕乔利（Luca Pacioli）所著的《算数、几何、比及比例概要》一书，是阐述复式记账法的第一本著作，也是近代会计史上的一个重要里程碑。复式记账法的产生在会计发展史上具有重大意义。经济学家熊彼特认为，资本主义起源于复式记账法，"资本主义实践将货币单位转换成为合理的成本—利润计算的工具，复式簿记是它高耸的纪念塔。"

3.5 Trial Balance 试算平衡表

After the December 20×8 transactions of Sun Financial Services have been recorded, the account balances are determined. The balances of the various T accounts at the end of December are the same as those shown in equation form.

小提示：

请注意，12 月末各 T 型账户的余额与会计等式中所列示的余额相同。一旦确定了账户余额，对账户余额的正确性就必须进行验证。

A statement to test the accuracy of the financial records is the **trial balance**. The trial balance is prepared to determine whether total debits equal total credits. When Sun Peng started Sun Financial Services with a cash investment, we said that property equaled financial interests. Using accounting terms, we stated that assets equal liabilities plus owner's equity. Later we saw that every entry on the debit, or left, side of one account is matched by an entry of equal amount on the credit, or right, side of another account.

知识点解析：

trial balance 试算平衡表。为验证总分类账中所有账户借方余额合计和贷方余额合计是否相等而编制的试算表。根据复式记账原理，当期所有账户的借方余额合计必须等于当期所有账户的贷方余额合计。试算表是对会计记录进行检查和验证的较为有效的方法，但试算表的平衡并不说明会计记录绝对正确，因为有些不影响借贷平衡关系的记账错误是试算表发现不了的，例如漏账、重复记账、借贷方向颠倒等。

The firm's financial records started with an equality of debits and credits and continued that equality in the recording process. It follows that the sum of the debit balances in the accounts should equal the sum of the credit balances. If the totals do not balance, that is, the total debit balances do not equal the total credit balances, it is clear that an error has been made. To prepare a trial balance, the balance of each account is first determined. Next, the account names and their balances are listed on a trial balance as shown in Table 3 – 5. The balance of each account is written in the proper debit or credit column. Debit balances are entered in the left column, and credit balances are entered in the right column.

Table 3 – 5 **A Trial Balance**

SUN FINANCIAL SERVICRS

Trial Balance

December 31, 20 ×8

Account Name	Debit	Credit
Cash	16 200	
Accounts Receivable	2 000	
Supplies	1 000	
Prepaid Rent	20 000	
Equipment	15 000	
Accounts Payable		4 000
Capital		40 000
Drawing	1 000	
Fees Income		14 000
Salaries Expense	2 500	
Utilities Expense	300	
Totals	58 000	58 000

小提示：

请注意，试算平衡表表头也要表明三方面内容：谁、什么和何时。试算平衡表的日期是会计期的期末，表中的账户按以下顺序列出：资产、负债、所有者权益、收入和费用。

3.6 Financial Statements 财务报表

After the account balances are determined and the trial balance prepared, the income statement, statement of owner's equity, and balance sheet are prepared. The income statement, statement of owner's equity and balance sheet for Sun Financial Services are presented in Table 3 – 6 to Table 3 – 8.

Table 3 - 6 **Income Statement for Sun Financial Services**

SUN FINANCIAL SERVICRS

Income Statement

Month Ended December 31, 20×8

Revenue		
Fees Income		14 000
Expenses		
Salaries Expense	2 500	
Utilities Expense	300	
Total Expenses		2 800
Net Income for the Month		11 200

Table 3 - 7 **Statement of Owner's Equity for Sun Financial Services**

SUN FINANCIAL SERVICRS

Statement of Owner's Equity

Month Ended December 31, 20×8

Capital, December 1, 20×8		40 000
Net Income for December	11 200	
Less Withdrawals for December	1 000	
Increase in Capital		10 200
Capital, December 31, 20×8		50 200

Table 3 - 8 **Balance Sheet for Sun Financial Services**

SUN FINANCIAL SERVICRS

Balance Sheet

December 31, 20×8

Assets		Liabilities	
Cash	16 200	Accounts Payable	4 000
Accounts Receivable	2 000		
Supplies	1 000		
Prepaid Rent	20 000	Owner's Equity	
Equipment	15 000	Capital	50 200
Total Assets	54 200	Total Liabilities and Owner's Equity	54 200

小提示：

请注意，利润表与所有者权益表的数据之间存在勾稽关系（articulation），所有者权益表与资产负债表的数据之间也存在勾稽关系。

3.7 Chart of Accounts 科目表

Since most businesses have many different accounts, it is necessary set up a system that allows the accounts to be easily identified and located. A **chart of accounts** is a list of all the accounts used by a business for recording its financial transactions. Each account is given a number as well as a name. The number is assigned on the basis of the type of account. Similar accounts are grouped within a certain block of numbers. For example, asset accounts could be numbered from 100 to 199, liability accounts from 200 to 299, owner's equity accounts from 300 to 399, and so on. These numbers help identify the type of account.

知识点解析：

chart of accounts 会计科目表，又称 code of accounts。会计科目表是系统地编列一个企业账户的名称和编号的一览表。我国有统一的会计制度，一级科目通常使用统一的名称和代码。国外的企业则可以自行制定自己的会计科目，大企业需要比较复杂的编号，如用 4 位数表示，而每位数字对分类均有特殊的意义。

Typically, accounts are numbered in the order in which they appear on the financial statements. The balance sheet accounts are listed first and then the income statement accounts, as illustrated in the chart of accounts shown in Table 3 – 9.

小提示：

请注意，这些科目并不是连续编号的。例如，资产类的编号从 101 到 111，然后跳到 121、131 和 141，以便在需要时添加其他账户。

Table 3 – 9 **Chart of Accounts**

SUN FINANCIAL SERVICRS
Chart of Accounts

Account Number	Account Name
Balance Sheet Accounts	
100 ~ 199	**ASSETS**
101	Cash
111	Accounts Receivable
121	Supplies
131	Prepaid Rent
141	Equipment
200 ~ 299	**LIABILITIES**
202	Accounts Payable
300 ~ 399	**OWNER'S EQUITY**
301	Capital
Statement of Owner's Equity Account	
302	Drawing
Income Statement Accounts	
400 ~ 499	**REVENUE**
401	Fees Income
500 ~ 599	**EXPENSES**
511	Salaries Expense
514	Utilities Expense

3.8 Permanent and Temporary Accounts 永久性账户与临时性账户

The asset, liability, and owner's equity accounts appear on the balance sheet at the end of an accounting period. The balances of these accounts are then carried forward to start the new period. Such accounts are sometimes called **permanent**, or **real**, **accounts** because they continue from accounting period to accounting period.

In contrast to these permanent accounts are the revenue, expense, and drawing accounts, whose balances are reported on the income statement and statements of owner's equity at the end of an accounting period. Accountants use revenue, expense, and drawing accounts to classify and summarize changes in owner's equity during the period. These accounts are called **temporary**, or **nominal**, **accounts** because their balances are transferred to the capital account at the end of an accounting period. The accounts then have zero balances and are ready for use in recording new transactions affecting revenue and expenses for the next period.

知识点解析：

permanent 永久性账户，又称实账户；temporary account 临时性账户，又称虚账户。永久性账户指资产负债表账户，每期期末的余额都将结转至下一个会计期间。临时性账户指利润表账户，由于它们是用来记录一个会计期间的收入和费用，确定该期间的经营成果，因此在一个会计期间结束时必须结清余额，以便在下一个会计期间从头开始记录该期间的收入和费用。

本章小结：

分析每项经济业务，在确定其对基本会计等式的影响后，要记录在恰当的账户中。使用T型账户记录经济业务时，要遵循“有借必有贷、借贷必相等”的记账规则。由于资产列示在会计等式的左边，资产的增加就记入资产类账户的左边，即借方。反之，资产的减少记入资产类账户的右边，即贷方。同理，负债列示在会计等式的右边。因此，负债的增加就记入负债类账户的右边，即贷方。反之，负债的减少记入负债类账户的左边，即借方。所有者权益类账户亦然。

收入类账户、费用类账户和个人提款账户都影响所有者权益。收入可增加所有者权益，即收入和使用者权益是同向变动的，因此，收入增加也记入收入类账户的贷方。费用会减少所有者权益，即费用和使用者权益是反向变动的，因此，费用增加记入费用类账户的借方。提款账户用于记录所有者从企业提取的资金，个人提款会减少所有者权益，其余额在所有者权益表中呈报。

会计科目表中，各类账户按特定顺序排列并编号，便于参考和查找。通常，会计科目按照其在财务报表中出现的顺序编号，资产负债表科目排在前面，接下来是利润表科目。

Self – Review & Questions 自测题

1. On which side of asset, liability and owner's equity accounts are increases recorded?

2. On which side of asset, liability and owner's equity accounts are decreases recorded?

3. What is meant by the normal balance of an account? Which are normal balance sides for asset, liability and owner's equity accounts?

4. What is the increase side for each of these accounts: Cash, Accounts Payable and Capital?

5. What are withdrawals and how are they recorded?

6. What is the main idea of double-entry accounting system?

7. What is a chart of accounts and what is its purpose?

8. What is a trial balance? When do accountants prepare the trial balance?

Translations 翻译题

Translate the following English into Chinese or Chinese into English.

1. Recording entries in accounts provides an efficient method of gathering data about the financial affairs of a business.

2. The income statement is prepared to report the revenue and expenses for the period and to determine the net income or loss.

3. The statement of owner's equity is prepared to analyze the change in owner's equity during the period.

4. The balance sheet summarizes the assets, liabilities, and owner's equity of the business on a given date.

5. The purpose of the chart of accounts is to provide a system by which the accounts of the business can be easily identified and located.

6. 复式记账法是指对任何一笔经济业务，都应以相等的金额，在两个或两个以上的账户中全面地、相互联系地进行登记的方法。

7. 资产负债表是用来列示企业的资产、负债和所有者权益，反映企业的财务状况的报表，也可称为财务状况表。

8. 利润表是通过将收入和费用配比，反映企业一定期间的经营成果，即净利润或净亏损。

Exercises 练习题

Exercise 3 – 1

Set up a T account for each account and enter the balance on the proper side of the account.

Cash	¥2 000
Equipment	¥2 000
Accounts Payable	¥1 000
Capital	¥3 000

Exercise 3 – 2

Bai Ying decided to start her dental practice. The first five transactions for the business are listed below. For each transaction, (1) determine which two accounts are affected, (2) set up T accounts for the affected accounts, and (3) enter the debit and credit amounts in the T accounts.

1. Bai Ying invested ¥20 000 cash in the business.
2. Paid ¥5 000 in cash for equipment.
3. Performed services for cash amounting to ¥2 000.
4. Paid ¥700 in cash for rent expense.
5. Paid ¥500 in cash for supplies.

Exercise 3 – 3

Determine whether the word *debit* or *credit* is correct for each space in the sentences below.

1. Asset accounts normally have ________ balances. These accounts increase on the ________ side and decrease on the ________ side.
2. Liability accounts normally have ________ balances. These accounts increase on the ________ side and decrease on the ________ side.
3. The owner's capital account normally has a ________ balance. This account increases on the ________ side and decreases on the ________ side.
4. Revenue accounts normally have ________ balances. These accounts increase on the ________ side and decrease on the ________ side.
5. Expense accounts normally have ________ balances. These accounts increase on the ________ side and decrease on the ________ side.

Exercise 3 – 4

Indicate whether each of the following accounts would normally have a debit balance or a credit balance.

1. Accounts Payable
2. Fees Income
3. Cash
4. Capital
5. Equipment
6. Accounts Receivable
7. Salaries Expense
8. Supplies

Exercise 3 – 5

Using T accounts to record transactions involving assets, liabilities, and owner's equity. The following transactions took place at Chen Remodeling Service.

Instructions:

Set up T accounts for the following accounts: Cash, Shop Equipment, Store Equipment, Truck, Accounts Payable, and Capital. Analyze each transaction carefully. Record the effects of the transaction in the T accounts.

Transactions:

1. Chen invested ¥10 000 cash in the business.
2. Purchased equipment for ¥500 in cash.
3. Bought store fixtures for ¥1 200; payment is due in 30 days.
4. Purchased a used truck for ¥2 500 in cash.
5. Chen gave the firm his personal set of tools costing ¥250.
6. Bought a used cash register for ¥200; payment is due in 30 days.
7. Paid ¥450 in cash to apply to the amount owed for store fixtures.
8. Chen withdrew ¥1 000 in cash for personal expenses.

Supplementary Reading 扩展阅读

The Importance of a Statement of Cash Flows

The published financial statements of corporations must include a statement of cash flows. The purpose of the statement of cash flows is to provide relevant information about the cash receipts and cash payments of a business entity during a fiscal period. Creditors (bondholders, noteholders, other lenders, and suppliers of goods and services) clearly look to a corporation's cash flows as the source for payment of interest and payment of debts. Investors who purchase stock in a corporation do so because they expect to receive a competitive rate of return on their investment. This return on investment is ultimately in the form of dividends, which are paid from corporate profits.

Management also is interested in cash flows. It must make plans to obtain cash to meet payrolls, to pay suppliers, and to meet other obligations. In planning future cash inflows and outflows, it is very helpful to analyze cash flows of the past. Past cash flows give an indication of the sources and uses of cash in the future.

Before the statement of cash flows is examined, it is necessary to understand the use of the word cash in the context of a statement of cash flows. The statement reflects both cash in the usual sense of the word and cash equivalents.

Cash and cash equivalents consist of currency, bank accounts, and short-term, highly liquid investments, such as certificates of deposit, that are easily convertible into known amounts of cash. Generally, if a short-term investment is to qualify as a cash equivalent, the investment must fall due within three months from the date the investment was acquired by the corporation. Thus a certificate of deposit acquired by a corporation on September 1, 20 ×8, and maturing on March 1, 20 ×9, would not be considered a cash equivalent on the December 31, 20 ×8, balance sheet because the maturity date is more than three months from the date the certificate was acquired.

In the statement of cash flows, cash receipts and cash payments must be classified under three general headings.

(1) Cash flows from operating activities. Routine business operations result in cash inflows and cash outflows. The most common transactions that give rise to cash inflows from operating activities include (a) the sale of merchandise or services for cash, (b) the collection of accounts receivable created by the sale of merchandise or services, and (c) miscellaneous sources, such as interest income. Similarly, cash outflows from operations commonly result from (a) paying expenses at the time they are incurred and (b) paying accounts payable created when merchandise is purchased or operating expenses are incurred and credited to accounts payable.

(2) Cash flows from investing activities. Investing activities are those transactions that involve the acquisition of assets (cash outflow) or disposal of assets (cash inflow) such as bonds of other corporations, land, buildings, and equipment. These assets are not purchased for resale and are not normally consumed in operations within one year.

(3) Cash flows from financing activities. Financing activities involve transactions between a corporation and those who provide cash to the corporation to carry on its activities. Note that interest expense is considered a part of operating, not financing activities.

The following financing activities result in cash inflows.

a. Issuing capital stock for cash
b. Issuing bonds for cash
c. Borrowing cash by issuing or discounting a note payable
d. Resale of treasury stock

The following financing activities result in cash outflows.

a. Paying a note payable or a bond payable
b. Purchasing treasury stock
c. Paying cash dividends on stock

CHAPTER 4 Journalizing and Posting 登记日记账与过账

本章学习目标

1. 掌握如何登记普通日记账。
2. 学会编制复合分录。
3. 掌握如何将普通日记账的会计数据过账记入总分类账。

本章核心术语

accounting cycle 会计循环
audit trail 审计线索
balance ledger form 余额式分类账
chronological order 序时记录
compound entry 复合分录
general journal 普通日记账
general ledger 总分类账
journal 日记账
journalizing 登记日记账
ledger 分类账
posting 过账

The analysis of each transaction is the basis for recording the effects of the transaction in the accounts. In business, written records are kept of each analysis for future reference. These records allow individuals to recheck their work and trace the details of any transaction long after it has happened.

The **accounting cycle** is a series if steps performed during each accounting period to classify, record and summarize data for a business and produce needed financial information. The first step in the accounting cycle is to analyze the effects of business transactions. The second step in the cycle is preparing a record of those transactions.

> **知识点解析：**
> accounting cycle 会计循环。会计循环指会计上按一定顺序处理业务的一套程序，即从确认应进入会计系统的交易和事件开始，经过登记日记账、过账记入分类账、编制各个阶段的试算平衡表直到编制财务报表的整个核算过程。

4.1 Journals 日记账

Business transactions are recorded in a financial record called a **journal**, which is a diary of business activities that lists events involving financial affairs—transactions—as they occur. The transactions are entered in **chronological order**—in the order in which they happen day by day.

Since the journal is the first accounting record where transactions are entered, it is sometimes referred to as a record of original entry. A number of different types of journals are used in business. The one that will be examined in this chapter is the general journal.

> **知识点解析：**
> journal 日记账，或称 book of original entry，day book of prime entry。指按经济业务发生的先后顺序，完整地记录经济业务发生的日期、所涉及的借贷方账户、金额以及经济业务摘要的账簿，它是经济业务的最初记录，以后要过账记到分类账中。

4.2 The General Journal 普通日记账

As its name implies, the **general journal** can be used to record all types of business transactions. The process of recording transactions in the general journal is referred to as **journalizing**. To illustrate how transactions are entered in this journal, let's start with the first transaction of Sun Financial Services.

When the owner, Sun Peng, invested ¥40 000 on November 6 to start the firm, the transaction was analyzed and the following effects identified.

a. Sun Financial Services received ¥40 000 of property in the form of cash.

b. Sun Peng had a ¥40 000 financial investment in the business.

Using this analysis as a guide, Zhang Hua, the office manager, knew that the accounting transaction should be entered as follows.

(1) Debit the Cash account for ¥40 000 to record the increase in the asset cash.

(2) Credit the Capital account for ¥40 000 to record the new ownership interest.

The written record of the analysis of the transaction appears in the general journal as Table 4 -1.

Table 4 -1 General Journal Entry for November 6

GENERAL JOURNAL PAGE 1

	Date		Description	Post. ref.	Debit	Credit
1	20×8					
2	Nov.	6	Cash		40 000	
3			Capital			40 000
4			Beginning investment			
5			of owner			
6						

小提示：

请注意，date 栏的填写要求：每一页记第一笔业务时，年、月、日要填写齐全，其余只填写日即可，只有当下一页开始，或年份、月份发生变化时，再填写年份和月份。每笔分录的日期都写在该笔分录第一行的 date 栏中。description 栏的填写要求：先记借方科目，借方金额记入同一行的 debit 栏；贷方科目记在借方科目的下一行，贷方金额记入同一行的 credit 栏；摘要应当完整而简洁，记入贷方科目的下一行。post. ref. 栏在日记账过账登记分类账时填写分类账的编号。

Whenever possible, the explanation for a journal entry should include a description of the source of the information contained in the entry. For example, if a check is written to make a payment, the explanation in the journal entry for that transaction should include the check number. Similarly, if goods are purchased on credit, the explanation in the journal entry should show the number of the supplier's invoice (bill). These source document numbers are part of an **audit trail**—a chain of references that makes it possible to trace information about transactions through the accounting system. The audit trail helps locate errors in the system. It also helps to prevent fraud because it provides a means of checking the data in a firm's financial records against the original data that appears in the source documents.

知识点解析：

audit trail 审计线索，又称审计轨迹。审计线索是审计师借以查明经济业务真相或数据生成过程的基本依据，是审计师获取审计证据的线索。在手工会计核算系统内，审计线索主要以书面记录的形式存在，主要表现在原始凭证→记账凭证→会计账簿→会计报表的流程之中。

Account titles are written in the general journal exactly as they appear in the chart of accounts and in the accounts themselves. Use of the exact wording of each account title minimizes the possibility of errors when the figures are transferred to the accounts. The transfer of information from the general journal to the accounts is the next step in the accounting process and is discussed later in this chapter.

4.2.1 General Journal Entries for November

The journal entries made at Sun Financial Services during November provide a good illustration of the techniques that are used to record transactions in the general journal. For example, on November 7 the firm paid ¥20 000 rent in advance for December through July. Analysis of the transaction and the journal entry are shown below (see Table 4-2).

(3) The business acquired a new asset (prepaid rent) at a cost of ¥20 000.

(4) The business paid ¥20 000 in cash.

Table 4-2　　General Journal Entry for November 7

GENERAL JOURNAL　　PAGE 1

	Date		Description	Post. ref.	Debit	Credit
6						
7	Nov.	7	Prepaid Rent		20 000	
8			Cash			20 000
9			Paid rent in advance for			
10			an eight-month period			

Continued

	Date		Description	Post. ref.	Debit	Credit
11			(December 20 ×8 through			
12			July 20 ×9), Check 1001			
13						

小提示：

请注意，在每一笔分录的摘要与下一笔分录之间应留有空行，这样使日记账的记录更明晰。另外，摘要中应写明原始凭证的编号，如支票（check）号、发票（invoice）号等，这是该笔业务审计线索的一部分，需要说明的是，本书的日记账示例大多对此做了省略。

When Sun Financial Services purchased equipment on November 9 for cash, the office manager made the following analysis and then recorded the journal entry that follows (see Table 4 –3).

(5) The firm purchased new assets in the form of equipment at a cost of ¥10 000.

(6) The firm paid ¥10 000 in cash.

Table 4 –3　　General Journal Entry for November 9

GENERAL JOURNAL　　PAGE 1

	Date		Description	Post. ref.	Debit	Credit
13						
14	Nov.	9	Equipment		10 000	
15			Cash			10 000
16			Purchased equipment			
17			Check 1002			
18						

On November 10 the business purchased a copy machine, a fax machine, calculators, and other necessary equipment for ¥5 000 on credit from ABC Corp., payable in 60 days. The transaction was analyzed and the journal entry was recorded as Table 4 –4.

(7) The business purchased new assets (equipment) at a cost of ¥5 000.

(8) The business owed ¥5 000 as an account payable to ABC Corp.

Table 4 – 4 General Journal Entry for November 10

GENERAL JOURNAL PAGE 1

	Date		Description	Post. ref.	Debit	Credit
18						
19	Nov.	10	Equipment		5 000	
20			Accounts Payable			5 000
21			Purchased equipment on			
22			credit from ABC Corp. ,			
23			payable in 60 days			
24						

On November 28, when the firm purchased supplies for ¥1 000 in cash, the transaction was analyzed and the journal entry was prepared as Table 4 – 5.

(9) The business purchased new assets (supplies) at a cost of ¥1 000.

(10) The business paid ¥1 000 in cash.

Table 4 – 5 General Journal Entry for November 28

GENERAL JOURNAL PAGE 1

	Date		Description	Post. ref.	Debit	Credit
24						
25	Nov.	28	Supplies		1 000	
26			Cash			1 000
27			Purchased supplies			
28						

A final transaction, the payment of purchased equipment for ¥1 000 by Cash to ABC Corp. , on November 30, was analyzed as shown and the journal entry that follows was made (see Table 4 – 6).

(11) The firm paid ¥1 000 in cash.

(12) ABC's claim against the firm was reduced by ¥1 000.

Table 4-6 **General Journal Entry for November 30**

GENERAL JOURNAL PAGE 1

	Date		Description	Post. ref.	Debit	Credit
28						
29	Nov.	30	Accounts Payable		1 000	
30			Cash			1 000
31			Paid ABC Corp., on			
32			account			
33						

4.2.2 General Journal Entries for December

You will recall that Sun Financial Services officially opened for business on December 1, 20×8. The following transactions were completed during that month. The journal entries made for these transactions provide a further illustration of the procedures used to record data in the general journal [Refer to items (13) through (24) in Chapter 3 to review the analysis of the December transactions].

1. Performed services for ¥10 500 in cash.
2. Performed services for ¥3 500 on credit.
3. Received ¥1 500 in cash from credit clients on their accounts.
4. Paid ¥2 500 for salaries.
5. Paid ¥300 for a utility bill.
6. The owner withdrew ¥1 000 for personal expenses.

The entries in the general journal are shown below. In actual practice the transactions involving revenue and cash received on account would be spread throughout the month and recorded as they occurred. However, for the sake of simplicity, these transactions have been summarized and recorded as of December 31 in Table 4-7.

Table 4-7 **General Journal Entries for December**

GENERAL JOURNAL PAGE 2

	Date		Description	Post. ref.	Debit	Credit
1	20×8					
2	Dec.	31	Cash		10 500	
3			Fees Income			10 500

Continued

	Date		Description	Post. ref.	Debit	Credit
4			Performed services for			
5			cash			
6						
7		31	Accounts Receivable		3 500	
8			Fees Income			3 500
9			Performed services on			
10			credit			
11						
12		31	Cash		1 500	
13			Account Receivable			1 500
14			Received cash from credit			
15			clients on account			
16						
17		31	Salaries Expense		2 500	
18			Cash			2 500
19			Paid monthly salaries to			
20			employee			
21						
22		31	Utilities Expense		300	
23			Cash			300
24			Paid monthly bill for			
25			utilities			
26						
27		31	Drawing		1 000	
28			Cash			1 000
29			Owner withdrew cash for			
30			personal expenses			
31						

4.2.3 Compound Entries

Each of the journal entries shown so far consists of a single debit and a single credit. However, some transactions require a **compound entry**—a journal entry that contains several debits or several credits. In a compound entry all debits are recorded first followed by the recording of the credits.

Suppose that when Sun Financial Services purchased the equipment on November 9 for ¥10 000, Sun Peng gave ¥5 000 in cash and agreed to pay the balance in 30 days. This transaction would be analyzed as follows.

1. An asset, Equipment, is increased by ¥10 000.
2. An asset, Cash, is decreased by ¥5 000.
3. A liability, Accounts Payable, is increased by ¥5 000.

The compound entry shown as Table 4 –8 would be enter in the general journal.

Table 4 –8 **General Journal Entry for the Compound Entry**

GENERAL JOURNAL PAGE 1

	Date		Description	Post. ref.	Debit	Credit
1	20×8					
2	Nov.	9	Equipment		10 000	
3			Cash			5 000
4			Accounts Payable			5 000
5			Purchased equipment on			
6			credit from ABC Corp.			
7			issued Check			
8			1002 for a ¥5 000 down			
9			payment; bal. due 30 days			
10						

Test your understanding

Make a compound journal entry for the following transaction: A firm purchases machinery for ¥3 000 with a cash down payment of ¥500 and with the balance payable in 30 days.

4.3 Ledgers 分类账

Although T accounts are a good device for quickly analyzing the effects of transactions, they are not suitable for use in business as financial records. With the journal as a guide, data about transactions can be entered in the accounts that are affected.

All the accounts together are referred to as a **ledger**. The process of transferring data from a journal to a ledger is known as **posting**. Because posting takes place after the transactions are journalized and the ledger is the last accounting record where a transaction is recorded, a ledger is sometimes called a **record of final entry**.

4.3.1 The General Ledger

One essential type of ledger for every business is the **general ledger**. This ledger is the master reference file for the accounting system because it provides a permanent, classified record of every financial element involved in a firm's operations. Many companies also have other kinds of ledgers that supplement the information in the general ledger.

知识点解析：

general ledger 总分类账。即以账户为分类标准所设置的整体性账户，分门别类登记记录于日记账上的经济业务。总分类账中的账户属于统驭账户，可与明细分类账户互相核对，便于查找记账错误。

4.3.2 Ledger Account Forms

Several different forms are available for general ledger accounts. The office manager for Sun Financial Services has decided to use a **balance ledger form** for the business's general ledger accounts. With this form the balance of an account is always available because it is recorded after each entry is posted. Table 4 –9 shows how data about the first transaction of the firm—the beginning investment of the owner—was posted from the general journal to the proper general ledger accounts.

Table 4-9 **Posting for the First Transaction**

GENERAL JOURNAL PAGE 1

	Date		Description	Post. ref.	Debit	Credit
1	20×8					
2	Nov.	6	Cash	101	40 000	
3			Capital	301		40 000
4			Beginning investment			
5			of owner			
6						

ACCOUNT Cash ACCOUNT NO. 101

Date		Explanation	Post. ref.	Debit	Credit	Balance	
						Debit	Credit
20×8							
Nov.	6		J1	40 000		40 000	

ACCOUNT Capital ACCOUNT NO. 301

Date		Explanation	Post. ref.	Debit	Credit	Balance	
						Debit	Credit
20×8							
Nov.	6		J1		40 000		40 000

4.3.3 Posting to the General Ledger

On November 7, 20×8, the office manager for Sun Financial Services made an entry in the general journal to record the payment of rent in advance for an eight-month period. Next, the data from the journal was posted to the proper account in the general ledger. The debit amount in the journal was transferred to the Debit column in the Prepaid Rent account and the credit amount in the journal was transferred to the Credit column in the Cash account (see Table 4-10).

Table 4 – 10 **Posting for the Second Transaction**

GENERAL JOURNAL PAGE 1

	Date		Description	Post. ref.	Debit	Credit
6						
7	Nov.	7	Prepaid Rent	131	20 000	
8			Cash	101		20 000
9			Paid rent in advance for			
10			an eight-month period			
11			(December 20 ×8 through			
12			July 20 ×9), Check 1001			
13						

ACCOUNT Prepaid Rent ACCOUNT NO. 131

Date		Explanation	Post. ref.	Debit	Credit	Balance	
						Debit	Credit
20 ×8							
Nov.	7		J1	20 000		20 000	

ACCOUNT Cash ACCOUNT NO. 101

Date		Explanation	Post. ref.	Debit	Credit	Balance	
						Debit	Credit
20 ×8							
Nov.	6		J1	40 000		40 000	
	7		J1		20 000	20 000	

小提示：

请注意，对于常规业务，分类账的摘要栏通常不必填写，除非特别需要说明的，因为日记账中已有较为详细的摘要。

The specific procedure used in posting data from a general journal entry is to start with the first account listed in the journal entry, in this example, Prepaid Rent. The general ledger account for Prepaid Rent is located and the following posting steps are taken:

(1) The date of the journal entry is recorded in the Date column of the ledger account.

(2) The number of the journal page is recorded in the Posting Reference column of the ledger account. For example, J1 is posted to the Prepaid Rent account to indicate that the entry was originally recorded on page 1 of the general journal. The letter J in front of the page number is an abbreviation for the general journal.

(3) The debit amount in the journal is recorded in the Debit column of the ledger account.

(4) The balance of the ledger account is determined and recorded in the Debit Balance column.

(5) The number of the ledger account is recorded in the Posting Reference column of the journal.

Similar steps are used to post the credit amount from the general journal entry to the Cash account. Once this work is done, the posting process for the transaction is complete and the journal entry includes the numbers of the two ledger accounts. Writing the journal page number in each ledger account and the ledger account number in the journal indicates that the entry has been posted and ensures against posting the same entry twice. The journal page numbers in the accounts and the account numbers in the journal provide a useful cross-reference when entries must be traced and transactions verified. Like the source document numbers that appear in the explanations for journal entries, posting references are part of the audit trail. These references allow accountants to trace an amount from the ledger to the proper journal entry and then to the source document that contains the original data.

After the office manager for Sun Financial Services had posted all the entries for November and December, the firm's general ledger accounts appeared as shown in Table 4－11.

Table 4－11 Posted General Ledger Accounts

ACCOUNT Cash ACCOUNT NO. 101

Date		Explanation	Post. ref.	Debit	Credit	Balance	
						Debit	Credit
20×8							
Nov.	6		J1	40 000		40 000	
	7		J1		20 000	20 000	
	9		J1		10 000	10 000	
	28		J1		1 000	9 000	
	30		J1		1 000	8 000	

Continued

Date		Explanation	Post. ref.	Debit	Credit	Balance	
						Debit	Credit
Dec.	31		J2	10 500		18 500	
	31		J2	1 500		20 000	
	31		J2		2 500	17 500	
	31		J2		300	17 200	
	31		J2		1 000	16 200	

ACCOUNT Accounts Receivable ACCOUNT NO. 111

Date		Explanation	Post. ref.	Debit	Credit	Balance	
						Debit	Credit
20×8							
Dec.	31		J2	3 500		3 500	
	31		J2		1 500	2 000	

ACCOUNT Supplies ACCOUNT NO. 121

Date		Explanation	Post. ref.	Debit	Credit	Balance	
						Debit	Credit
20×8							
Nov.	28		J1	1 000		1 000	

ACCOUNT Prepaid Rent ACCOUNT NO. 131

Date		Explanation	Post. ref.	Debit	Credit	Balance	
						Debit	Credit
20×8							
Nov.	7		J1	20 000		20 000	

ACCOUNT Equipment ACCOUNT NO. 141

Date		Explanation	Post. ref.	Debit	Credit	Balance	
						Debit	Credit
20×8							
Nov.	9		J1	10 000		10 000	
	10		J1	5 000		15 000	

ACCOUNT Accounts Payable ACCOUNT NO. 202

Date		Explanation	Post. ref.	Debit	Credit	Balance	
						Debit	Credit
20×8							
Nov.	10		J1		5 000		5 000
	30		J1	1 000			4 000

ACCOUNT Capital ACCOUNT NO. 301

Date		Explanation	Post. ref.	Debit	Credit	Balance	
						Debit	Credit
20×8							
Nov.	6		J1		40 000		40 000

ACCOUNT Drawing ACCOUNT NO. 302

Date		Explanation	Post. ref.	Debit	Credit	Balance	
						Debit	Credit
20×8							
Dec.	31		J1	1 000		1 000	

ACCOUNT Fees Income ACCOUNT NO. 401

Date		Explanation	Post. ref.	Debit	Credit	Balance	
						Debit	Credit
20×8							
Dec.	31		J2		10 500		10 500
	31		J2		3 500		14 000

ACCOUNT Salaries Expense ACCOUNT NO. 511

Date		Explanation	Post. ref.	Debit	Credit	Balance	
						Debit	Credit
20×8							
Dec.	31		J2	2 500		2 500	

ACCOUNT Utilities Expense ACCOUNT NO. 514

Date		Explanation	Post. ref.	Debit	Credit	Balance	
						Debit	Credit
20×8							
Dec.	31		J2	300		300	

As you can see, each ledger account provides a complete running history of the increases and decreases in the item that it represents. When a balance ledger form is used, the account also shows the current balance for the account at all times.

The general ledger accounts are usually arranged so that the balance sheet accounts—assets, liabilities, and owner's equity—come first. The accounts for the income statement come next, with the revenue accounts first, followed by the expense accounts. The numbering system used in the chart of accounts follows the same order. This arrangement speeds the preparation of the trial balance, the income statement, the statement of owner's equity, and the balance sheet. All figures are found in the general ledger in the order in which they will be presented on the financial statements.

本章小结：

日记账是一种全面反映每项经济业务的序时记录，在日记账中进行记录的过程称为记日记账。记日记账时，先记借方科目与金额，再记贷方科目与金额，并附有摘要，以便建立审计线索。

过账是会计数据从日记账转移到分类账中的过程。分类账是用于分门别类反映资产、负债、所有者权益、收入和费用等账户金额增减变化的账簿。日记账和分类账的编号也构成审计线索，它们可以相互核对，以检查过账的正确性。

Self – Review & Questions 自测题

1. Why is the journal referred to as the "record of original entry"?

2. Transactions are entered in the general journal in chronological order. What does this mean?

3. Why are check and invoice numbers included in the journal entry explanation?

4. If a compound journal entry has two accounts debited, will there always be two accounts credited?

5. What is a ledger? Discuss its functions.

6. Why is the ledger called the "record of final entry"?

7. What is recorded in the posting reference column of a balance ledger form?

8. What is recorded in the posting reference column of the general journal?

9. What is the purpose of writing the posting reference in each ledger account and the ledger account number in the journal?

Translations 翻译题

Translate the following English into Chinese or Chinese into English.

1. A well-run accounting system also provides for prompt and accurate journalizing of all transactions. It also provides for timely and accurate posting of data to the ledger accounts.

2. Since management uses this information for the decision making, it is essential that the statements be prepared quickly at the end of each period and that they contain the correct figures.

3. A journal contains a chronological (day-by-day) record of a firm's transactions. Each entry provides a written analysis of a transaction, showing what accounts should be debited and credited and the amounts involved.

4. The firm should be able to trace amounts through the accounting records and back to their origin-the source documents on which the transactions were first recorded.

5. Data is transferred from the journal entries to the ledger accounts through a process called posting. The information that appears in the financial statements is taken from the general ledger.

6. 账户是对会计要素各具体内容进行的分类反映和控制。

7. 日记账是按业务发生的先后顺序记录的。

8. 历史成本是指企业拥有的各项资产应当以取得时实际发生的成本入账。

Exercises 练习题

Exercise 4 – 1

Selected accounts from the general ledger of the Popular Design Studio are shown below. Record the general journal entries that would be made to record the following transactions. Be sure to include dates and explanations in these entries.

101 Cash
111 Accounts Receivable
121 Supplies
131 Equipment
141 Automobile
202 Accounts Payable
301 Capital
302 Drawing
401 Fees Income
511 Rent Expense
514 Salaries Expense
517 Telephone Expense
520 Automobile Expense

Transactions:

(1) Sept. 1 Zhao Tian invested ￥38 000 in cash to start the firm.

(2) Sept. 4 Purchased office equipment for ￥8 700 on credit, which is payable in 30 days.

(3) Sept. 16 Purchased an automobile that will be used to visit clients; issued check for ￥15 600 in full payment.

(4) Sept. 20 Purchased supplies for ￥175; paid immediately with check.

(5) Sept. 23 Returned damaged supplies and received a cash refund of ￥75.

(6) Sept. 30 Issued Check for ￥4 200 as payment on account.

(7) Sept. 30 Withdrew ￥1 500 in cash for personal expenses.

(8) Sept. 30 Issued Check for ￥800 to pay the rent for October.

(9) Sept. 30 Performed services for ¥1 275 in cash.

(10) Sept. 30 Issued Check for ¥125 to pay the monthly telephone bill.

Exercise 4 –2

Post the journal entries that you prepared for Popular Design Studio in Exercise 4 –1 from the general journal to the general ledge. Use the accounting title shown in Exercise 4 –1.

Exercise 4 –3

Reflected below are five transactions for Central Air Conditioning Service that occurred during December 20 ×8, the first month of operation. Record the transactions in the general journal and post them to the appropriate ledger accounts. Be sure to number the journal page 1 and to write the year at the top of the Date column. Use the account titles and numbers listed below.

101 Cash
111 Accounts Receivable
121 Office Supplies
131 Tools
141 Machinery
151 Equipment
161 Truck
202 Accounts Payable
301 Capital
401 Fees Income

Transactions:

(1) Dec. 1 Xu Dong invested ¥15 000 in cash plus tools with a fair market value of ¥800 to start the business.

(2) Dec. 2 Purchased equipment for ¥1 800 and office supplies for ¥200; issued Check for ¥500 as a down payment with the balance due in 30 days.

(3) Dec. 10 Performed services for ¥1 200, received ¥600 in cash with the balance due in 30 days.

(4) Dec. 15 Purchased a truck for ¥14 000; issued check for ¥4 000 as a cash down payment with the balance due in 90 days.

(5) Dec. 20 Purchased machinery for ¥1 500; issued check for ¥500 as a cash down payment with the balance due in 30 days.

Supplementary Reading 扩展阅读

Full Disclosure in Financial Reporting

The most common types of disclosure include four sections:

1. The Financial Statements

This section contains the most relevant and significant information about the corporation expressed in quantitative terms, and the form and arrangement of the financial statements should ensure that the most vital information is readily apparent and understandable to the financial statement users. It consists of balance sheet, income statement, and the statement of cash flows.

2. Footnotes to the Financial Statements

This section are the accountant's means of amplifying or explaining the items presented in the main body of the statements. It presents the information that cannot be easily incorporated into the financial statements, and it usually includes: (1) schedules and exhibits such as long-term debt, (2) explanations of financial statement items such as receivables, inventories, and investment, and (3) general information about the company such as subsequent events, contingencies, and relevant trade. Examples of notes are: descriptions of the accounting policies and methods used in measuring the elements reported in the statements; explanations of uncertainties and contingencies; and statistics and details too voluminous to be included in the statements.

3. The Auditor's Opinion

This section is a form of disclosure in that it informs users of the reliability of the financial statements. An auditor is an accounting professional who conducts an independent examination of the accounting data presented by a business enterprise. An unqualified opinion indicates more reliable financial statements than does a qualified or adverse opinion, because the unqualified opinion means that the financial statements present the financial position, results of operations, and cash flows fairly in accordance with accounting standards.

4. Management's Discussion and Analysis

This section presents the information relative to liquidity, capital resources, and the results of operations. The management required to mention the favorable and unfavorable trends, significant events and uncertainties affecting these three factors.

CHAPTER 5 The Worksheet and Adjustments 工作底稿与账项调整

本章学习目标

1. 掌握如何在工作底稿中进行试算平衡。
2. 理解会计期末为何要进行调整，并掌握调整分录的编制。
3. 掌握如何编制工作底稿。
4. 掌握如何从工作底稿中生成利润表、所有者权益表和资产负债表。
5. 掌握如何将调整分录记入日记账并过账。

本章核心术语

account form balance sheet 账户式资产负债表
adjusting entries 调整分录
book value 账面价值
contra asset account 资产备抵账户
depreciation 折旧
prepaid expenses 预付费用
report form balance sheet 报告式资产负债表
salvage value 残值
straight-line depreciation 直线法
worksheet 工作底稿（表）

After all the transactions for the operating period are posted to the ledger accounts, the trial balance is prepared to test the accuracy of the financial records. Because management will use the financial statements to make decisions, every effort must be made to ensure that these reports contain no errors.

5.1 The Worksheet 工作底稿

When the trial balance shows that the general ledger is in balance, the financial statements for the period are prepared. These statements must be completed as soon as possible if they are to be useful. Therefore, anything that can be done to save time is important. One way to prepare the financial statements more quickly is by using a form called a worksheet. A **worksheet** is an accounting form with many columns that is used to gather all the data needed at the end of an accounting period to prepare the financial statements.

A common type of worksheet is shown in Table 5 – 1. The worksheet contains 10 money columns, which are arranged in five sections labeled Trial Balance, Adjustments, Adjusted Trial Balance, Income Statement, and Balance Sheet. Each section includes a Debit column and a Credit column.

Table 5 – 1 **Ten-column Worksheet**

SUN FINANCIAL SERVICRS
Worksheet
Month Ended December 31, 20 ×8

Account Name	Trial Balance		Adjustments		Adjusted Trial Balance		Income Statement		Balance Sheet	
	Dr.	Cr.	Dr.	Cr.	Dr.	Cr.	Dr.	Cr.	Dr.	Cr.

知识点解析：

worksheet 工作底稿（表），又称 working sheet 或 working paper，是会计人员用以整理数据、编制财务报表的底稿，既有助于财务报表的编制，也有助于全面了解企业会计的决算程序和过程。通常，工作底稿由十个借贷方栏目组成，其中包括试算平衡表借贷方栏、调整分录借贷方栏、调整后试算平衡表借贷方栏、利润表项目借贷方栏和资产负债表项目借贷方栏。工作底稿完成后，编制财务报表所需数据便已齐全。

审计中也使用工作底稿一词，指注册会计师用于记录审计过程、审计程序和审计证据等的书面资料，是编写审计报告的主要依据，也是检查审计工作质量的依据，必要时可作为法庭证实或解脱注册会计师责任的依据。

 5.1.1 The Trial Balance Section

To save time and effort, many accountants prepare the trial balance on the worksheet. They list the general ledger accounts directly on the worksheet and then transfer the balances from the general ledger to the Debit and Credit columns of the Trial Balance section. After the account balances are recorded on the worksheet, the equality of the debits and credits is proved by totaling the Debit and Credit columns. The Trial Balance columns must have equal debit and credit totals, as you can see in Table 5－2.

Table 5－2　A Partial Worksheet

SUN FINANCIAL SERVICRS
Worksheet (Partial)
Month Ended December 31, 20×8

Account Name	Trial Balance		Adjustments	
	Dr.	Cr.	Dr.	Cr.
Cash	16 200			
Accounts Receivable	2 000			
Supplies	1 000			(a) 500
Prepaid Rent	20 000			(b) 2 500
Equipment	15 000			
Accumulates Depreciation—Equipment				(c) 250
Accounts Payable		4 000		
Capital		40 000		
Drawing	1 000			
Fees Income		14 000		
Salaries Expense	2 500			
Utilities Expense	300			
Supplies Expense			(a) 500	
Rent Expense			(b) 2 500	
Depreciation Expense—Equipment			(c) 250	
Totals	58 000	58 000	3 250	3 250

Examine the Trial Balance section of the partial worksheet in Table 5－2. Zhang Hua, the office manager for Sun Financial Services, has added four new accounts to the firm's general ledger: Accumulated Depreciation—Equipment, Supplies Expense, Rent Expense and Depreciation Expense—Equipment. These accounts do not have balances yet, but they will be needed as other parts of the worksheet are prepared. Zhang Hua has therefore listed them in the Trial Balance section so that they can appear in numeric order with the rest of the general ledger accounts. The use of these new accounts will be explained in the discussion of the Adjustments section of the worksheet that follows.

5.1.2 The Adjustments Section

Most changes in a firm's account balances are caused by transactions between the business and another business or individual. In the case of Sun Financial Services, all the changes in its accounts discussed so far were caused by transactions that the firm had with suppliers, customers, the landlord, and employees. These changes were easy to recognize and were journalized and posted as they occurred. However, some changes are not caused by transactions with other businesses or individuals. Instead, they arise from the internal operations of the firm itself, and they must be recognized and recorded at the end of each accounting period. The worksheet provides a convenient form for gathering the information and determining the effects of the changes on the accounts involved.

知识点解析：

adjusting entries 调整分录。调整分录是由权责发生制所要求的，只在会计期末所做的有关应计和摊销等的会计分录，如计提折旧、计列应计费用、计提坏账准备等。

The process of updating accounts at the end of an accounting period for previously unrecorded items that belong to the period is referred to as making **adjustments**, or **adjusting entries**. Let's look at the adjustments made at Sun Financial Services on December 31, 20×8, the end of the business's first month of operations, to get a more detailed picture of the process.

Test your understanding

Adjusting entries are (　　).

A. not necessary if the accounting system is operating properly

B. usually required before financial statements are prepared

C. made whenever management desires to change an account balance

D. made to balance sheet accounts only

Adjustments for Supplies Used

On November 28, 20×8, Sun Financial Services purchased supplies for ¥1 000. Some of these supplies were used during December in the course of operations. However, on the December 31 trial balance, the Supplies account still shows a balance of ¥1 000. In order to present an accurate and complete picture of the firm's financial affairs at the end of December, an adjustment must be made for the supplies used. Otherwise, the asset account Supplies will be overstated because fewer supplies are actually on hand. Similarly, the firm's expenses will be understated because the cost of supplies used represents an operating expense that has not been recorded.

On December 31, 20×8, Zhang Hua made a count of the remaining supplies and found that they totaled ¥500. This meant that supplies amounting to ¥500 were used during the month (¥1 000 - ¥500 = ¥500). Analysis of this situation shows the following effects on the firm's accounts.

1. The Supplies Expense account has increased by ¥500.
2. The Supplies account has decreased by ¥500.

Both the debit and credit of the adjustment are labeled (a) as shown in Table 5-2. Identifying the two parts of an adjustment is especially helpful when the adjustments are journalized after the worksheet has been completed.

Test your understanding

A firm paid ¥450 for supplies during the accounting period. At the end of the accounting period the firm had ¥200 of supplies on hand. What information is entered on the worksheet to show this adjustment?

Adjustment for Expired Rent

On November 7, 20×8, Sun Financial Services paid ¥20 000 rent in advance for an eight-month period (December 20×8 through July 20×9). As a result of this transaction, the firm acquired the right to occupy facilities for the specified period. Since the right is considered a form of property, the ¥20 000 was debited to an asset account called Prepaid Rent. On December 31, 20×8, the firm's trial balance still shows a balance of ¥20 000 in this account. However, the firm has used up part of its right to occupy the facilities—one month of the prepaid rent has expired.

Since the ¥20 000 sum covered an eight-month period, the expired rent for December amounts to ¥2 500(1/8 of ¥20 000 = ¥2 500). Thus on December 31 the asset account Prepaid Rent is overstated by ¥2 500. At the same time the firm's expense are understated because the ¥2 500 expired rent represents an operating expense that has not been recorded. The cost of facilities used (rent) is a cost of doing business.

To update the accounts involved, an adjustment is made on December 31. The effect of this adjustment are as follows.

1. The Rent Expense account has increased by ¥2 500.
2. The Prepaid Rent account has decreased by ¥2 500.

These two figures are labeled (b) as shown in the Adjustments section of the partial worksheet in Table 5 – 2.

Supplies and prepaid rent are known as **prepaid expenses**. They are expense items that are acquired and paid for in advance of their use. As you have seen, at the time of their acquisition, these items represent assets for a business and are therefore recorded in asset accounts. However, as they are used, their cost is transferred to expense accounts by means of adjusting entries at the end of each accounting period.

Other common prepaid expenses are prepaid insurance and prepaid advertising. These items are debited to the asset accounts Prepaid Insurance and Prepaid Advertising when they are acquired. Later the expired cost that applies to each accounting period is debited to Insurance Expense and Advertising Expense and credited to the asset accounts in end-of-period adjusting entries.

Test your understanding

A firm paid ¥6 000 for a six-months fire insurance policy on January 1, 20×8. What is the necessary adjustment for insurance expense at the end of the first month of the accounting period?

Adjustments for Depreciation

One other adjustment must be made for Sun Financial Services at the end of December 20×8, its first month of operations. On November 9 and November 10 the firm purchased equipment at a total cost of ¥15 000. This equipment was put to use in December when the firm opened for business. At the time the equipment was bought, its cost was debited to the asset account Equipment. On December 31, 20×8, the firm's trial balance therefore shows a balance of ¥15 000 in the Equipment account.

The various items of equipment that were purchased all have an estimated useful life of five years and no expected salvage value after that period. **Salvage value** is the amount an item can be sold for after its use by the business. Because long-term assets like the firm's equipment help to earn revenue for a business, their cost is charged to operations (transferred to expense) as they are used. This charge is made at the end of each accounting period by means of an adjusting entry. The process of allocating the cost of a long-term asset to operations during its expected useful life is known as **depreciation**. There are many different ways to determine the amount of depreciation to charge to expense in each accounting period. The method that Zhang Hua has decided on is a very simple and widely used one called **straight-line depreciation**. Under this method, depreciation is computed by the formula:

Depreciation = (Cost − Salvage value)/ Estimated months of useful life

This formula results in an equal amount of depreciation being charged to each accounting period during the asset's useful life.

Since the equipment purchased by Sun Financial Services is expected to have a useful life of five years and no salvage value, its entire cost of ¥15 000 must be depreciated over the five-year period. The amount of depreciation for December 20×8, the first month of operations, is computed as follows.

1. convert the asset's useful life from years to months: 5×12 months =60 months.

2. the total depreciation to be taken is divided by the total number of months: ¥15 000/60 = ¥250.

3. The amount of depreciation to be charged off for December 20×8 and every other month during the asset's useful life is ¥250.

知识点解析：

straight-line depreciation 直线法折旧。这种计算折旧方法假定固定资产在其寿命期内的使用状况是均衡的，提供的服务是等同的，所以将固定资产的成本平均地分配到它的使用期间里。直线法计算最为简便，应用也极广泛。

As the cost of the equipment is gradually transferred to expense, its **book value** (recorded value) as an asset must be reduced. This procedure cannot be carried out by directly decreasing the ¥15 000 balance in the asset account Equipment. Accounting principles require that the original cost of a long-term asset continue to appear in the asset account until the firm has used up or disposed of the asset. Thus another account called Accumulated Depreciation—Equipment is used to keep a record of the total depreciation taken and to reduce the book value of the asset.

知识点解析：

book value 账面价值，又称 carrying value。泛指反映于账簿上的金额，其中包括一切资产、负债和所有者权益项目的金额。当该词汇用于固定资产时，通常是指固定资产的净值，即由原始价值减去累计折旧。一个企业的账面价值是指企业的资产总值超过负债总值的余额。账面价值并不一定与市场价值相符，由于物价的不断上涨，企业资产的账面价值（即历史成本）往往与其现实价值存在相当大的差异。

Accumulated Depreciation—Equipment is a special type of account called a **contra asset account**. The account has a credit balance, which is contrary, or opposite, to the normal balance of an asset account. The credit balance is subtracted from the debit balance of the Equipment account on the balance sheet to report the book value of the asset.

知识点解析：

contra asset account 抵消资产账户，又称备抵账户。用于抵消某些资产账户的余额，从而反映资产的净值，如累计折旧和坏账准备等账户。

The effects of the adjustment for depreciation at Sun Financial Services on December 31, 20×8, are as follows.

1. Depreciation Expense—Equipment has increased by ¥250.
2. Accumulated Depreciation—Equipment has increased by ¥250.

These figures are labeled (c) on the partial worksheet in Table 5－2.

Test your understanding

A firm purchases machinery, which has an estimated useful life of 10 years and no salvage value, for ¥12 000 at the beginning of the accounting period. What is the adjusting entry for depreciation at the end of one month if the firm uses the straight-line method of depreciation?

If the firm had other kinds of long-term assets, an adjustment for depreciation would be made for each one. Typical long-term assets owned by business in addition to equipment are land, buildings, trucks, automobiles, furniture and fixtures. Of these items, only land is not subject to depreciation.

知识点解析：

furniture and fixtures 家具与装置，家具指办公室所需的桌、椅、办公柜等器具；装置指室内吊灯、吸音板等设施。

After the adjustment for depreciation of the equipment is recorded on the worksheet of the firm, the Adjustments columns are totaled. The totals of the Debit and Credit columns in this section must be equal. If they are not, Zhang Hua must locate and correct the error or errors before continuing. Examine the partial worksheet in Table 5 – 2 to see how the Adjustments section was completed.

Test your understanding

If an accountant forgot to record depreciation on office equipment at the end of an accounting period, which of the following would be true regarding the statements prepared at that time?

A. The assets are overstated and owner's equity is understated

B. The assets and owner's equity are both understated

C. The assets are overstated, net profit is understated, and owner's equity is overstated

D. The assets, net profit, and owner's equity are overstated

5.1.3 The Adjusted Trial Balance Section

The next task is to prepare an adjusted trial balance using the worksheet. This process involves two steps:

1. combine the figures from the Trial Balance section and the Adjustments section to record the updated account balances in the Adjusted Trial Balance section.

2. check on the equality of the debits and credits of the combined figures before extending the balances to the financial statement sections.

Refer to the Adjusted Trial Balance section of the partial worksheet shown in Table 5 –3.

Table 5 –3 **Partial Worksheet**

SUN FINANCIAL SERVICRS
Worksheet (Partial)
Month Ended December 31, 20 ×8

Account Name	Trial Balance		Adjustments		Adjusted Trial Balance	
	Dr.	Cr.	Dr.	Cr.	Dr.	Cr.
Cash	16 200				16 200	
Accounts Receivable	2 000				2 000	
Supplies	1 000			(a) 500	500	
Prepaid Rent	20 000			(b) 2 500	17 500	
Equipment	15 000				15 000	
Accumulates Depreciation—Equipment				(c) 250		250
Accounts Payable		4 000				4 000
Capital		40 000				40 000
Drawing	1 000				1 000	
Fees Income		14 000				14 000
Salaries Expense	2 500				2 500	
Utilities Expense	300				300	
Supplies Expense			(a) 500		500	
Rent Expense			(b) 2 500		2 500	
Depreciation Expense—Equipment			(c) 250		250	
Totals	58 000	58 000	3 250	3 250	58 250	58 250

When figures must be combined to calculate updated account balances for the adjusted trial balance, follow these rules.

1. If an account has a debit balance in the Trial Balance section and there is a debit entry in the Adjustments section, add the two amounts.

2. If an account has a debit balance in the Trial Balance section and there is a credit entry in the Adjustments section, subtract the credit amount.

3. If an account has a credit balance in the Trial Balance section and there is a credit entry in the Adjustments section, add the two amounts.

4. If an account has a credit balance in the Trial Balance section and there is a debit en-

try in the Adjustments section, subtract the debit amount.

知识点解析：

adjusted trial balance 调整后试算平衡表，即完成调整分录之后，为了及早发现在将调整分录登记到日记账和过账的过程中发生的差错，在编制财务报表之前再编制一份余额试算。

The other accounts affected by adjustments (Accumulated Depreciation—Equipment, Supplies Expense, Rent Expense and Depreciation Expense—Equipment) had no balances when the Trial Balance section of the worksheet was prepared. Thus the figures shown in the Adjustments section are extended to the Adjusted Trial Balance section. For example, the ¥250 credit entry for Accumulated Depreciation—Equipment is recorded as the balance of that account in the Credit column of the Adjusted Trial Balance section.

Once all account balances have been recorded in the Adjusted Trial Balance section, the Debit and Credit columns are totaled. Just as with the original trial balance, the adjusted trial balance must have equal debit and credit totals. If these totals are not equal, the errors must be located. It is essential that all figures be correct before they are used to complete the financial statement sections of the worksheet.

5.1.4 The Income Statement and Balance Sheet Sections

The Income Statement and Balance Sheet sections of the worksheet are used to organize the figures needed for these financial reports. For example, to prepare an income statement, all the revenue and expense account balances must be in one place. It is convenient to assemble this information on the worksheet.

The process of completing the financial statement sections is quite simple. Starting at the top of the Adjusted Trial Balance section, each general ledger account is examined. If an account will appear on the balance sheet, the amount is entered in the Balance Sheet section. If an account will appear on the income statement, the amount is entered in the Income Statement section. When amounts are extended from the Adjusted Trial Balance section to the statement sections, every effort should be made not to enter a debit amount in the Credit column or a credit amount in the Debit column.

The Balance Sheet Section

Remember that the general ledger accounts are numbered according to type in the following sequence: assets, liabilities, owner's equity, revenue and expenses. The accounts appear on the worksheet in this order. Thus the first five accounts in the Adjusted Trial Balance section of the partial worksheet shown in Table 5 – 4 are assets. They are extended to the Debit column of the Balance Sheet section.

Table 5 – 4 **Partial Worksheet**

SUN FINANCIAL SERVICRS
Worksheet (Partial)
Month Ended December 31, 20 ×8

Account Name	Adjusted Trial Balance		Income Statement		Balance Sheet	
	Dr.	Cr.	Dr.	Cr.	Dr.	Cr.
Cash	16 200				16 200	
Accounts Receivable	2 000				2 000	
Supplies	500				500	
Prepaid Rent	17 500				17 500	
Equipment	15 000				15 000	
Accumulates Depreciation—Equipment		250				250
Accounts Payable		4 000				4 000
Capital		40 000				40 000
Drawing	1 000				1 000	
Fees Income		14 000		14 000		
Salaries Expense	2 500		2 500			
Utilities Expense	300		300			
Supplies Expense	500		500			
Rent Expense	2 500		2 500			
Depreciation Expense—Equipment	250		250			
Totals	58 250	58 250	6 050	14 000	52 200	44 250
Net Income			7 950			7 950
			14 000	14 000	52 200	52 200

The next three accounts in the Adjusted Trial Balance section have credit balances. They are a contra asset account (Accumulated Depreciation—Equipment), a liability account (Accounts Payable) and an owner's equity account (Capital). The balances of these accounts are extended to the Credit column of the Balance Sheet section. The account, Drawing, has a debit balance that is extended to the Debit column of the Balance Sheet section, as shown in Table 5 –4.

The Income Statement Section

All revenue and expense accounts must appear on the income statement. Thus the credit balance of the Fees Income account is extended to the Credit column of the Income Statement section of the worksheet. The last five accounts in the Adjusted Trial Balance section are expense accounts. The debit balances of these accounts are extended to the Debit column of the Income Statement section, as shown in Table 5 –4.

After all account balances have been transferred from the Adjusted Trial Balance section of the worksheet to the financial statement sections, the columns in the Income Statement section are totaled. In the Income Statement columns of the worksheet for Sun Financial Services, the debits (expenses) total ¥6 050 and the credits (revenue) total ¥14 000.

Next the columns in the Balance Sheet section are totaled. As shown in Table 5 –4, the debits (assets and drawing account) total ¥52 200 and the credits (contra asset, liabilities and owner's equity) total ¥44 250.

Since the Income Statement columns include all revenue and expenses, the totals of these columns are used to determine the net income or net loss. The smaller column total is subtracted from the larger one. In this case the total of the Credit column, ¥14 000, which represents the revenue, exceeds the total of the Debit column, ¥6 050, which represents the expenses. The difference between the two amounts is a net income of ¥7 950.

The net income causes a net increase in owner's equity as a result of the firm's operations for the month. As a check on accuracy, the amount in the Balance Sheet Debit column is subtracted from that in the Credit column and compared to net income. If the amounts are the same, the amount of net income is added to the Credit column of the Balance Sheet section of the worksheet. The net income is also recorded on the worksheet below the total of the Debit column of the Income Statement section. The words "Net Income" are entered to identify the amount.

After the net income is recorded on the worksheet, the Income Statement and Balance Sheet columns are totaled again. All pairs of columns should then be in balance. The partial worksheet prepared at Sun Financial Services on December 31, 20×8, is shown in Table 5 –4.

If the business had a loss, *Net Loss* would be entered on the worksheet and the amount of loss entered in the Credit column of the Income Statement section and the Debit column of the Balance Sheet section.

5.2 Preparing Financial Statements 编制财务报表

All the figures needed to prepare the financial statements are now properly organized on the worksheet. The accounts are arranged in the order in which they must appear on the income statement and the balance sheet. The net income (or loss) has been determined for use in preparing the statement of owner's equity. The next step is to prepare the income statement.

5.2.1 The Income Statement

The income statement is prepared directly from the data in the Income Statement section of the worksheet. Compare the income statement for Sun Financial Services shown in Table 5 – 5 with the worksheet in Table 5 – 4.

Table 5 – 5 **Income Statement**

SUN FINANCIAL SERVICRS
Income Statement
Month Ended December 31, 20×8

Revenue		
Fees Income		14 000
Expenses		
Salaries Expense	2 500	
Utilities Expense	300	
Supplies Expense	500	
Rent Expense	2 500	
Depreciation Expense—Equipment	250	
Total Expenses		6 050
Net Income for the Month		7 950

If the firm had incurred a net loss, the final amount on the income statement would be labeled "Net Loss".

5.2.2 The Statement of Owner's Equity

The statement of owner's equity is prepared from the data in the Balance Sheet section of the worksheet. The statement of owner's equity is prepared before the balance sheet so that the amount of the ending capital balance is available for presentation on the balance sheet. As previously discussed, the statement of owner's equity reports the changes that have occurred in the owner's financial interest during the reporting period. The statement of owner's equity for Sun Financial Services is shown in Table 5 -6.

Table 5 -6 Statement of Owner's Equity

SUN FINANCIAL SERVICRS
Statement of Owner's Equity
Month Ended December 31, 20 ×8

Capital, December 1, 20 ×8		40 000
Net Income for December	7 950	
Less Withdrawals for December	1 000	
Increase in Capital		6 950
Capital, December 31, 20 ×8		46 950

5. 2. 3 The Balance Sheet

The accounts listed on the balance sheet are taken directly from the Balance Sheet section of the worksheet. The balance sheet for Sun Financial Services is shown in Table 5 -7.

Table 5 -7 Balance Sheet

SUN FINANCIAL SERVICRS
Balance Sheet
December 31, 20 ×8

Assets		
Cash		16 200
Accounts Receivable		2 000
Supplies		500
Prepaid Rent		17 500
Equipment	15 000	
Less Accumulated Depreciation	250	14 750
Total Assets		50 950
Liabilities and Owner's Equity		
Liabilities		

Continued

Accounts Payable		4 000
Owner's Equity		
Capital		46 950
Total Liabilities and Owner's Equity		50 950

Notice how the equipment is reported on the balance sheet. Three figures are shown in connection with this item—the original cost of ¥15 000, the accumulated depreciation of ¥250, and the book value of ¥14 750. The book value is computed by subtracting the accumulated depreciation from the original cost. The book value should not be confused with the market value. The market value may be higher or lower.

This type of balance sheet called the **report form**. Unlike the **account form**, which was illustrated in Chapters 2 and 3, the report form lists the liabilities and owner's equity under the assets rather than to the right of them. The report form is widely used because it provides more space for entering account titles and its format is easier to prepare.

小提示：

请注意，我国企业会计准则要求资产负债表采用账户式，账户式中资产与权益之间的恒等关系更一目了然。报告式的资产负债表在国外用的比较广泛，报告式也便于编制比较资产负债表。

5.3 Adjusting Entries 调整分录

As previously discussed, the worksheet is a tool that helps to determine the effects of adjustments on account balances and to prepare the financial statements. After the statements are completed, it is necessary to create a permanent record of any changes in account balances that are shown on the worksheet. These changes are recorded through adjusting entries made in the general journal and then posted to the general ledger. To see how the process works, let's consider again the financial affairs of Sun Financial Services on December 31, 20×8, the end of its first month of operations.

When the worksheet for December was prepared, the firm's office manager decided that three adjustments were necessary to provide a complete and accurate picture of the business operating results and its financial position. Adjustments were made for supplies used, expired rent, and depreciation on the equipment that the business owns. Each adjustment must now be journalized and posted to the general ledger accounts. The entries are made in the order in which the adjustments appear on the worksheet. Refer to the partial worksheet in Table 5 – 3 and the explanations given in the text for each of the items that appear there.

Many accountants prefer to separate the adjusting entries from the routine entries that are recorded throughout the accounting period. One common method is to write the heading "Adjusting Entries" in the Description column of the general journal on the line above the first adjusting entry. This procedure was used by Sun Financial Services. Some accountants also prefer to start a new page when they record the adjusting entries.

As soon as all adjusting entries are recorded in the general journal, the entries are posted to the general ledger. Refer to Table 5 – 8 to see how the adjusting entries made at Sun Financial Services on December 31, 20 ×8, were journalized and posted. Account numbers appear in the general journal because all the entries have been posted.

小提示:

请注意，为了与日常业务分录有所区别，调整分录记入日记账时，在 description 栏需先写明"Adjusting Entries"字样；或另起一页进行记录。同时，在分类账的 explanation 栏也应写明"Adjusting"字样。

Table 5 – 8　　Journalized and Posted Adjusting Entries

GENERAL JOURNAL　　PAGE 3

	Date		Description	Post. ref.	Debit	Credit
1	20 ×8		Adjusting Entries			
2	Dec.	31	Supplies Expense	517	500	
3			Supplies	121		500
4						
5		31	Rent Expense	520	2 500	
6			Prepaid Rent	131		2 500
7						
8		31	Depr. Expense – Equipment	523	250	
9			Accum. Depr. – Equipment	142		250
10						

ACCOUNT Supplies ACCOUNT NO. 121

Date		Explanation	Post. ref.	Debit	Credit	Balance	
						Debit	Credit
20×8							
Nov.	28		J1	1 000		1 000	
Dec.	31	Adjusting	J3		500	500	

ACCOUNT Prepaid Rent ACCOUNT NO. 131

Date		Explanation	Post. ref.	Debit	Credit	Balance	
						Debit	Credit
20×8							
Nov.	7		J1	20 000		20 000	
Dec.	31	Adjusting	J3		2 500	17 500	

ACCOUNT Accumulated Depreciation—Equipment ACCOUNT NO. 142

Date		Explanation	Post. ref.	Debit	Credit	Balance	
						Debit	Credit
20×8							
Dec.	31	Adjusting	J3		250		250

ACCOUNT Supplies Expense ACCOUNT NO. 517

Date		Explanation	Post. ref.	Debit	Credit	Balance	
						Debit	Credit
20×8							
Dec.	31	Adjusting	J3	500		500	

ACCOUNT Rent Expense ACCOUNT NO. 520

Date		Explanation	Post. ref.	Debit	Credit	Balance	
						Debit	Credit
20×8							
Dec.	31	Adjusting	J3	2 500		2 500	

ACCOUNT Depreciation Expense—Equipment ACCOUNT NO. 523

Date		Explanation	Post. ref.	Debit	Credit	Balance	
						Debit	Credit
20×8							
Dec.	31	Adjusting	J3	250		250	

本章小结：

通常情况下，编制工作底稿可以节约编制财务报表的时间。编制工作底稿和财务报表的程序依次为：在工作底稿上进行试算平衡；登记调整分录；编制调整后的试算平衡，再次验证调整后各借方合计与贷方合计相等；将利润表和资产负债表各项目金额分别计入相应栏目；确定净收入或净损失，并完成工作底稿；编制利润表，所有者权益表和资产负债表；将工作底稿“调整”栏中的调整分录记入日记账，并过账到总分类账中。

预付费用和折旧是其中需要调整的两个项目。预付费用是指在使用前已购买并支付，购买时将其反映为资产记录在资产账户中，使用时其成本通过会计期末的调整分录转化为费用。折旧是将固定资产的成本在其预期使用寿命内进行分配的过程，直线法是一种广泛使用的折旧方法。

Self – Review & Questions 自测题

1. Why is the worksheet prepared?
2. What are adjustments?
3. What accounting element does a prepaid expense represent?
4. Why are prepaid items adjusted at the end of an accounting period?
5. Explain the uses of the trial balance.
6. Describe the difference between a trial balance and an adjusted trial balance.
7. Why is the net income for a period recorded in the Balance Sheet section of the worksheet as well as the Income Statement section?
8. How does a balance sheet in the report form differ from a balance sheet in the account form?
9. Why is it necessary to journalize and post adjusting entries even though the data is already recorded on the worksheet?

Translations 翻译题

Translate the following English into Chinese or Chinese into English.

1. The use of a worksheet permits quicker preparation of the financial statements. Thus management can obtain necessary information when it is still timely.

2. The data recorded in a firm's accounting records is checked at the end of the operating period, adjusted for certain items that were not recorded during the period, and summarized in financial statements.

3. The more accounts that a firm has in its general ledger, the more useful the worksheet is in speeding up the preparation of the financial statements.

4. It is important to management that the appropriate adjustments are recorded. Otherwise, the financial statements will not present a complete and accurate picture of the firm's financial affairs.

5. Preparing financial statements is one of the accountant's most important jobs. All figures must be checked and double-checked to make sure they are accurate.

6. 调整分录记录资产或负债的变化，同时也涉及利润表账户。

7. 试算平衡表不仅能验证总分类账户借贷方记录的平衡性，还为财务报表的编制打下基础，但也存在一定的局限性。

8. 费用分为资本性支出和收益性支出，它们的区别在于影响几个会计期间，还是只影响当前的会计期间。

Exercises 练习题

Exercise 5 – 1

Determine the necessary adjustments for each of the following situations.

1. On June 1, 20×8, a new firm paid ¥6 000 rent in advance for a six-month period. The ¥6 000 was debited to the Prepaid Rent account.

2. On June 1, 20×8, the firm purchased supplies for ¥1 075. The ¥1 075 was debited to the Supplies account. An inventory of supplies at the end of June showed that items costing ¥560 were on hand.

3. On June 1, 20×8, the firm purchased equipment costing ¥6 000. The equipment is expected to have a useful life of five years and no salvage value. The firm will use the

straight-line method of depreciation.

Exercise 5 – 2

For each of the following situations, determine the necessary adjustments.

1. A firm purchased a two-year insurance policy for ¥2 400 on July 1, 20 ×8. The ¥2 400 was debited to the Prepaid Insurance account. What adjustment should be made to record expired insurance on the firm's July 31, 20 ×8, worksheet?

2. On December 1, 20 ×8, a firm signed a contract with a local radio station for advertising that will extend over a one-year period. The firm paid ¥2 040 in advance and debited the amount to Prepaid Advertising. What adjustment should be made to record expired advertising on the firm's December 31, 20 ×8, worksheet?

Exercise 5 – 3

On January 31, 20 ×8, the general ledger of a company showed the following account balances. Prepare the worksheet through the Adjusted Trail Balance section. Assume that every account has the normal debit or credit balance. The worksheet covers the month of January.

Accounts	Balance
Cash	9 500
Accounts Receivable	3 200
Supplies	1 500
Prepaid Insurance	2 850
Equipment	15 930
Accumulated Depreciation—Equipment	
Accounts Payable	1 700
Capital	18 900
Fees Income	15 000
Rent Expense	1 200
Salaries Expense	1 420
Supplies Expense	
Insurance Expense	
Depreciation Expense—Equipment	

Additional Information:

a. On January 31, 20 ×8, supplies used during the month totaled ¥800.

b. Expired insurance totaled ¥250.

c. Depreciation expense for the month was ¥230.

Case Analysis 案例分析

You have been hired as an "accounting consultant" by Watson Company to evaluate its financial reporting policies. Watson is a small corporation with a few stockholders owning stock that is not publicly traded. In a discussion with you, Chris Watson, the company president, says "For the Watson Company's annual income statement, it is our policy to always record and report revenues when we collect the cash and to record and report expenses when we pay the cash. I like this approach, and I think our stockholders and creditors do, too. This policy results in income that is reliable and conservative which is the way accounting should be. Besides, it is easy to keep track of our income. All I need are the receipts and payments recorded in the company's checkbook."

(Source: Bazley Nikolai Jones. Intermediate Accounting，余恕莲改编，高等教育出版社，2016.)

From financial reporting and ethical perspectives, how would you reply to Chris?

CHAPTER 6 Closing Entries and the Accounting Cycle 结账分录与会计循环

本章学习目标

1. 掌握如何将结账分录记入日记账并过账。
2. 学会编制结账后的试算平衡表。
3. 能够解释财务报表中会计数据的经济含义。
4. 了解会计循环的步骤。

本章核心术语

closing entries　结账分录
Income Summary account　收益汇总账户
post-closing trial balance　结账后试算平衡表

Once the worksheet and financial statements are completed, the general ledger must be updated by recording and posting the adjusting entries. As you have learned, the purpose of recording and posting the adjusting entries is to create a permanent record of the adjustments that appear on the worksheet. The next step is to journalize the entries that transfer the results of operations to owner's equity and prepare the revenue and expense accounts for use in the next accounting period.

6.1 Closing Entries 结账分录

Closing entries are journal entries that transfer the results of operations (the net income or net loss for the period) to owner's equity and reduce the balances of the revenue and expense accounts to zero so that they are ready to receive data for the next period. Like adjusting entries, closing entries are made in the general journal.

知识点解析：

closing entries 结账分录。即将本期的临时性账户余额变为零的会计分录。需要通过结账分录完成结转的账户有各收入类账户、费用类账户和收益汇总账户。如果企业使用股利账户的话，还要结转股利账户。

6.1.1 The Income Summary Account

A special owner's equity account called **Income Summary** is used to summarize the results of operations in the general ledger. It is used only at the end of a period to help with the closing procedure. The account has no balance after the closing process, and it remains without a balance until the closing procedure for the next period.

The Income Summary account is classified as a temporary owner's equity account. Other titles sometimes used for this account are *Revenue and Expense Summary* and *Income and Expense Summary*.

知识点解析：

Income Summary account 收益汇总账户。收益汇总账户是国外会计在期末结账时使用的一个汇总账户，其借方反映本期的费用，贷方反映本期的收入，余额便是本期的经营成果，借方余额为亏损，贷方余额为利润。该账户为过渡性账户，期末应将其余额进行结转。

6.1.2 The Closing Process

The closing process is accomplished by performing the four steps reflected below:

1. The balance of the revenue account is transferred to the Income Summary account.
2. The balances of the expense accounts are transferred to the Income Summary account.
3. The balance of the Income Summary account is transferred to the Capital account.
4. The balance of the Drawing account is closed to the Capital account.

Step 1: Transferring revenue account balances

On December 31, 20×8, the worksheet for Sun Financial Services shows a credit balance of ¥14 000 in the Fees Income account. This balance represents the total revenue for the period.

To close an account is simply to reduce its balance to zero. Since the Fees Income account has a credit balance, the account is debited for the same amount, which closes it. The offsetting credit is made to the Income Summary account. The effects of this closing entry are to transfer the total revenue for the period to the Income Summary account and to reduce the balance of the revenue account to zero.

Many accountants prefer to separate the closing entries from other types of journal entries. One common method is to write "Closing Entries" in the Description column of the general journal on the line above the first closing entry.

Step 2: Transferring expense account balances

The Income Statement section of Sun Financial Service's worksheet lists five expense accounts and shows that the total of their balances is ¥6 050. Since the expense accounts have debit balances, a credit is entered in each account to close it. A compound entry in the general journal is made to close the expense accounts. The total of the expenses is debited to the Income Summary account, and each expense accounts is credited for the amount of its balance. The effects of this closing entry are to transfer the total of the expenses for the period to the Income Summary account and to reduce the balances of the expense accounts to zero.

When the journal entries are posted, the words "Closing Entries" are written in the Explanation column of the individual revenue and expense accounts to identify clearly the closing entries in the general ledger. Similarly, notations are often made in the Explanation column of the Income Summary account to identify entries.

Test your understanding

A firm has the following expenses and revenue: Salaries Expense, ¥1 680; Supplies Expense, ¥320; Rent Expense, ¥800; and Fees Income, ¥18 000. Give the entry to close the expense and revenue accounts.

Step 3: Transferring net income or net loss to owner's equity

The next step in the closing procedure is to transfer the balance of Income Summary to the owner's capital account. On December 31, 20×8, the Income Summary account had a credit balance of ¥7 950. This balance represents the net income for the month (revenue of ¥14 000 minus expenses of ¥6 050). The general journal entry to record the transfer of the net income is a debit of ¥7 950 to the Income Summary account and a credit of ¥7 950 to the Capital account.

When this entry is posted, the balance of the Income Summary account is reduced to zero and the owner's capital account is increased by the amount of the net income.

Step 4: Transferring the Drawing account balance to Capital

You will recall that withdrawals are funds taken from the business by the owner for personal use. Withdrawals are recorded in the Drawing account. Withdrawals are not expenses of the business but are decreases in the owner's equity in the business. Since withdrawals are not expenses, they do not affect net income or net loss. Withdrawals are recorded in the Drawing account and appear in the statement of owner's equity as a deduction from Capital. Therefore, the Drawing account is closed directly to the Capital account.

After this entry is posted, the new balance of the Capital account agrees with the final amount listed in the Owner's Equity section of the balance sheet for December 31, 20×8.

After the closing entries for Sun Financial Services are posted to general ledger accounts, the general journal and ledger accounts appear as shown in Table 6-1.

Table 6-1 The Closing Process Completed: General Journal and General Ledger

GENERAL JOURNAL PAGE 4

	Date		Description	Post. ref.	Debit	Credit
1	20×8		Closing Entries			
2	Dec.	31	Fees Income		14 000	
3			Income Summary			14 000
4						
5			Income Summary		6 050	
6			Salaries Expense			2 500
7			Utilities Expense			300
8			Supplies Expense			500
9			Rent Expense			2 500
10			Depreciation Expense—equipment			250
11						
12			Income Summary		7 950	
13			Capital			7 950
14						

Continued

	Date		Description	Post. ref.	Debit	Credit
15			Capital		1 000	
16			Drawing			1 000
17						

ACCOUNT Capital ACCOUNT NO. 301

Date		Explanation	Post. ref.	Debit	Credit	Balance	
						Debit	Credit
20×8							
Nov.	6		J1		40 000		40 000
Dec.	31	Closing	J4		7 950		47 950
	31	Closing	J4	1 000			46 950

ACCOUNT Drawing ACCOUNT NO. 302

Date		Explanation	Post. ref.	Debit	Credit	Balance	
						Debit	Credit
20×8							
Dec.	31		J2	1 000		1 000	
Dec.	31	Closing	J4		1 000	0	

ACCOUNT Income Summary ACCOUNT NO. 399

Date		Explanation	Post. ref.	Debit	Credit	Balance	
						Debit	Credit
20×8							
Dec.	31	Closing	J4		14 000		14 000
Dec.	31	Closing	J4	6 050			7 950
	31	Closing	J4	7 950			0

ACCOUNT Fees Income ACCOUNT NO. 401

Date		Explanation	Post. ref.	Debit	Credit	Balance	
						Debit	Credit
20×8							
Dec.	31		J2		10 500		10 500
Dec.	31		J2		3 500		14 000
	31	Closing	J4	14 000			0

ACCOUNT Salaries Expense ACCOUNT NO. 511

Date		Explanation	Post. ref.	Debit	Credit	Balance	
						Debit	Credit
20×8							
Dec.	31		J2	2 500		2 500	
Dec.	31	Closing	J4		2 500	0	

ACCOUNT Utilities Expense ACCOUNT NO. 514

Date		Explanation	Post. ref.	Debit	Credit	Balance	
						Debit	Credit
20×8							
Dec.	31		J2	300		300	
Dec.	31	Closing	J4		300	0	

ACCOUNT Supplies Expense ACCOUNT NO. 517

Date		Explanation	Post. ref.	Debit	Credit	Balance	
						Debit	Credit
20×8							
Dec.	31	Adjusting	J3	500		500	
Dec.	31	Closing	J4		500	0	

ACCOUNT Rent Expense ACCOUNT NO. 520

Date		Explanation	Post. ref.	Debit	Credit	Balance	
						Debit	Credit
20×8							
Dec.	31	Adjusting	J3	2 500		2 500	
Dec.	31	Closing	J4		2 500	0	

ACCOUNT Depreciation Expense—Equipment ACCOUNT NO. 523

Date		Explanation	Post. ref.	Debit	Credit	Balance	
						Debit	Credit
20×8							
Dec.	31	Adjusting	J3	250		250	
Dec.	31	Closing	J4		250	0	

6.2 Post-closing Trial Balance 结账后试算平衡表

Every effort must be made to avoid mistakes in the general ledger at the start of the new accounting period. These mistakes may arise from errors made in recording the adjusting and closing entries. If such errors occur, the general ledger will not balance at the end of the new period and it could be time-consuming to find the errors.

The post-closing trial balance, or *after-closing trial balance*, is prepared to test the equality of total debits and credits and is the last step in the end-of-period routine. Only the accounts with balances are listed on a post-closing trial balance. These accounts—the assets, liabilities and owner's Capital accounts—are permanent and remain open at the end of the period. If the post-closing trial balance totals are equal, you can safely proceed with the recording of entries for the new period. The post-closing trial balance prepared for Sun Financial Services on December 31, 20×8, is shown Table 6-2.

知识点解析：

post-closing trial balance 结账后试算平衡表。结账分录也要记入日记账并过记到分类账，为了验证结账过程无差错，结账分录过账后要编制一份余额试算表，这个余额试算表就被称为结账后试算表。

Table 6 – 2 **Post-closing Trial Balance**

SUN FINANCIAL SERVICES
Post-closing Trial Balance
December 31, 20×8

Account name	Debit	Credit
Cash	16 200	
Accounts Receivable	2 000	
Supplies	500	
Prepaid Rent	17 500	
Equipment	15 000	
Accumulates Depreciation—Equipment		250
Accounts Payable		4 000
Capital		46 950
Totals	51 200	51 200

6.3 Interpreting the Financial Statements 解读财务报表

The last step in the accounting cycle is interpreting the financial statements. Management must have timely and accurate financial information to operate the business successfully. Information obtained from the financial statements assists management in achieving this objective by providing the answers to many questions, including:

- How much cash does the business have?
- How much money do customers owe the business?
- What is the amount owed to suppliers?
- How much profit did the firm make?

The financial statements for Sun Financial Services at the end of its first accounting period are shown in Table 6 – 3 to Table 6 – 5. By interpreting these statements, management can see that:

- The business has ¥16 200 in cash.
- The business is owed ¥2 000 by its customers.
- The business owes ¥4 000 to its suppliers.
- The business has made a profit of ¥7 950.

Table 6-3　　End-of-month Income Statement

SUN FINANCIAL SERVICES
Income Statement
Month Ended December 31, 20×8

Revenue		
Fees Income		14 000
Expense		
Salaries Expense	2 500	
Utilities Expense	300	
Supplies Expense	500	
Rent Expenses	2 500	
Depreciation Expense—Equipment	250	
Total Expenses		6 050
Net Income for the Month		7 950

Table 6-4　　End-of-month Statement of Owner's Equity

SUN FINANCIAL SERVICRS
Statement of Owner's Equity
Month Ended December 31, 20×8

Capital December 1, 20×8		40 000
Net Income for December	7 950	
Less Withdrawals for December	1 000	
Increase in Capital		6 950
Capital, December 31, 20×8		46 950

Table 6-5　　End-of-month Balance Sheet

SUN FINANCIAL SERVICES
Balance Sheet
December 31, 20×8

Assets		
Cash		16 200
Accounts Receivable		2 000
Supplies		500
Prepaid Rent		17 500
Equipment	15 000	
Less Accumulated Depreciation	250	14 750

Continued

Total Assets		50 950
Liabilities and Owner's Equity		
Liabilities		
Accounts Payable		4 000
Owner's Equity		
Capital		46 950
Total Liabilities and Owner's Equity		50 950

6.4 The Accounting Cycle 会计循环

You have now learned that the accounting cycle is a series of steps performed during each fiscal period to classify, record and summarize financial data for a business to produce needed financial information. You learned about the entire accounting cycle as you studied the financial affairs of Sun Financial Services during the first month of its operations. The steps in this cycle are summarized in Figure 6 – 1.

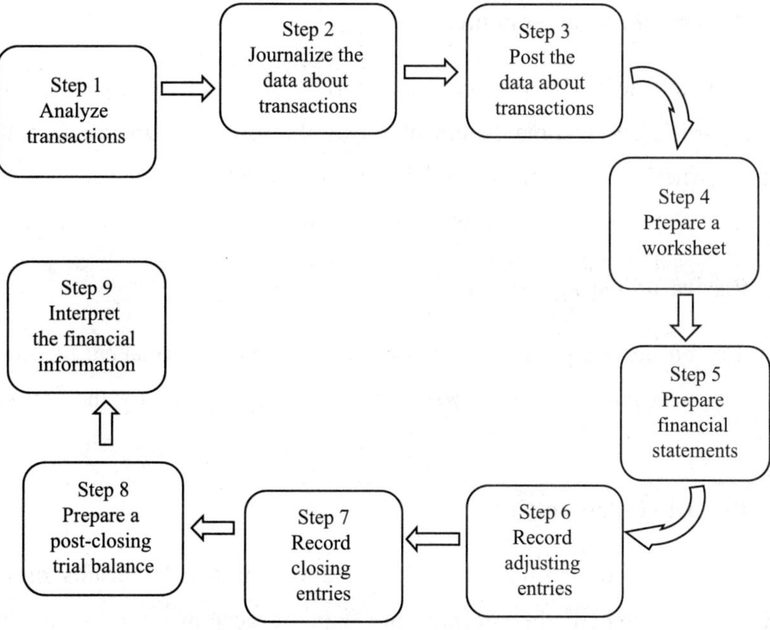

Figure 6 – 1 The Accounting Cycle

Step 1: Analyze transactions

The data about transactions appears on a variety of source documents—sales slips, purchase invoices, credit memorandums, check stubs, and so on. These source documents are analyzed to determine their effects on the basic accounting equation.

Step 2: Journalize the data about transactions

The effects of the transactions are recorded in a journal.

Step 3: Post the data about transactions

The data about transactions is transferred from the journal entries to the ledger accounts.

Step 4: Prepare a worksheet

At the end of each period of operations, a worksheet is prepared. The Trial Balance section is used to prove the equality of total debits and credits in the general ledger. The Adjustments section is used to enter changes in account balances that may be needed to present a more accurate and complete picture of the firm's financial affairs. The Adjusted Trial Balance section provides a check on the equality of debits and credits after adjustments are made. The Income Statement and Balance Sheet sections provide data to prepare financial statements.

Step 5: Prepare financial statements

The financial statements are prepared to report information to owners, managers, and other interested parties. The income statement shows the results of operations for the period, the statement of owner's equity reports the changes in the owner's financial interest, and the balance sheet shows the financial position of the business at the end of the period.

Step 6: Record adjusting entries

The adjusting entries are journalized and posted to create a permanent record of the changes in account balances made on the worksheet when the adjustment for the period were determined.

Step 7: Record closing entries

The closing entries are journalized and posted to transfer the results of operations to owner's equity and to prepare the revenue and expense accounts for use in the next period. The closing entries reduce the balances of the revenue, expense and Drawing accounts to zero.

Step 8: Prepare a post-closing trial balance

Another trial balance is prepared to make sure the general ledger is in balance after the adjusting and closing entries are posted.

Step 9: Interpret the financial information

Accountants, owners, managers and other interested parties interpret financial statements by comparing such things as profit, revenue and expenses from one accounting period to the next.

After studying the accounting cycle of Sun Financial Services, you have an understanding of how data flows through a simple accounting system for a small business. The data that comes into the system by means of source documents is analyzed; recorded in the general journal; posted to the general ledger; proved, adjusted and summarized on the worksheet; and then reported on financial statements. This data flow is illustrated in Figure 6 –2.

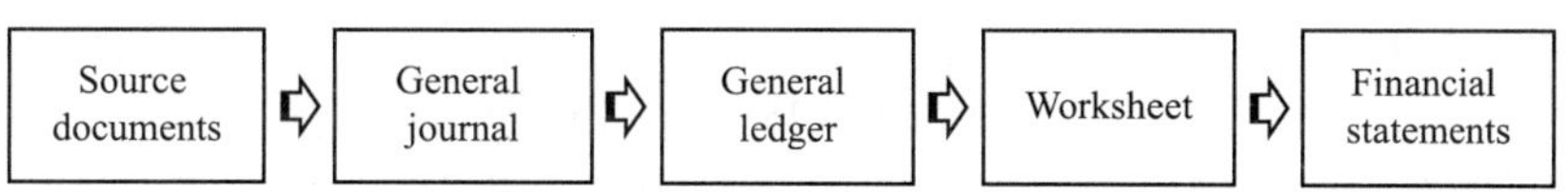

Figure 6 –2 The Flow of Data through a Simple Accounting System

You will familiar with accounting systems that have more complex records, procedures and financial statements. However, keep in mind that the steps of accounting cycle remain the same and the underlying accounting principles also remain the same.

本章小结：

会计循环是每个会计期间周而复始的一系列会计工作。期末完成工作底稿和财务报表，并将调整分录记入日记账并过账后，要将结账分录记入日记账，并编制结账后试算平衡表。结账分录需要使用一个过渡性账户，即“收益汇总”。收入和费用账户的余额结转到该账户，收益汇总账户的余额表示该期间的净收入或净损失，该余额要结转到所有者权益的资本账户。期末，提款账户也要进行结转。结账分录过账后，收入和费用账户清零，为汇总下一个会计期间的数据做准备。

结账后试算平衡表用于验证结账后所有总分类账户的借方余额合计和贷方余额合计是否相等，结账后试算平衡表中列示的是期末仍保留余额的永久性账户，即资产类、负债类和所有者类的资本账户。

Self – Review & Questions 自测题

1. What type account is Income Summary?
2. What are the four steps in the closing process?
3. Why are revenue and expense accounts called temporary?
4. What is the purpose of closing entries? When are they made?
5. What entry is made to close the Drawing account?
6. Why is a post-closing trial balance prepared?
7. What accounts appear on the post-closing trial balance?
8. What are the first three steps in the accounting cycle?
9. What three financial statements are prepared during the accounting cycle?
10. List and describe the steps in the accounting cycle.

Translations 翻译题

Translate the following English into Chinese or Chinese into English.

1. Although management is not involved in the details of day-to-day accounting procedures, the efficiency of the procedures has a major effect on the quality and promptness of the financial information that management receives.

2. After the closing entries are posted, the Capital account reflects the results of operations for the period, and the revenue and expense accounts have zero balances.

3. If the firm has more revenue than expenses, a net income is reported for the period. If the firm has more expenses than revenue, a net loss is reported.

4. The post-closing trial balance lists only the permanent accounts that remain open at the end of the period—the asset, liability, and owner's Capital accounts.

5. The accounting cycle consists of a series of steps that are repeated in each fiscal period. These steps are designed to classify, record, and summarize financial data for a business to produce needed financial information.

6. 资产负债表账户均属于永久性账户，资产、负债和所有者权益的账户余额在期末不需结清。

7. 财务报表是会计信息系统的最终“产品”，可分为月度、季度、半年度和年度财务报表。

8. 财务报表的主要目的是帮助决策者评估企业的经济实力、盈利能力及发展前景。

Exercises 练习题

Exercise 6 – 1

Managers often consult financial statements for specific types of information. Indicate whether each of the following items of information would appear on the income statement, statement of owner's equity, or the balance sheet. Use *I* for the income statement, *E* for the statement of owner's equity, and *B* for the balance sheet. If an item appears on more than one statement, use all letters that apply to that item.

1. Cash on hand.
2. Revenue earned during the period.
3. Total assets of the business.
4. Net income for the period.
5. Owner's capital at the end of the period.
6. Supplies on hand.
7. Cost of supplies used during the period.
8. Accounts receivable of the business.
9. Accumulated depreciation on the firm's equipment.
10. Amount of depreciation charged off on the firm's equipment during the period.
11. Original cost of the firm's equipment.
12. Book value of the firm's equipment.
13. Total expenses for the period.
14. Accounts payable of the business.
15. Owner's withdrawals for the period.

Exercise 6 – 2

The ledger accounts of a real estate company appear as follows on March 31, 20×8. All of the accounts have normal balances. Journalize and post the closing entries. Use J4 as the page number for the general journal in journalizing the closing entries.

Account NO.	Account	Balance
101	Cash	11 500
111	Accounts Receivable	2 200
121	Supplies	1 350

Continued

Account NO.	Account	Balance
131	Prepaid Insurance	3 480
141	Equipment	16 800
142	Accum. Depr. —Equipment	3 360
202	Accounts Payable	1 800
301	Capital	19 600
302	Drawing	1 000
404	Fees Income	46 000
510	Rent Expense	4 800
511	Salaries Expense	23 600
514	Utilities Expense	1 200
517	Supplies Expense	650
518	Telephone Expense	900
519	Insurance Expense	1 600
523	Depr. Expense—Equipment	1 680

Exercise 6 – 3

A commercial laundry, owned by Chen Lan, provides service to hotels, motels, and hospitals. On January 31, 20 ×8, the firm's worksheet showed the adjustment data given below. The balances of the revenue and expense accounts listed in the Income Statement section of the worksheet and the Drawing account listed in the Balance Sheet section of the worksheet are also given.

Adjustments:

a. Supplies used, ¥1 430.

b. Expired insurance, ¥185.

c. Depreciation on machinery, ¥560.

Account NO.	Account	Balance
302	Drawing	1 200 Dr.
404	Fees Income	16 400 Cr.
511	Rent Expense	1 500 Dr.
514	Salaries Expense	8 000 Dr.
517	Utilities Expense	320 Dr.

Continued

Account NO.	Account	Balance
520	Telephone Expense	105 Dr.
523	Supplies Expense	1 430 Dr.
526	Insurance Expense	185 Dr.
529	Depr. Expense—Machinery	560 Dr.

Instructions:

1. Record adjusting entries in the general journal.
2. Record closing entries in the general journal.

Case Analysis 案例分析

You are the accountant for Spaedy Company and are preparing the financial statements for 20×8. Near the end of 20×8, Spaedy Company loaned its president ¥100 000 because she was having financial difficulties. The note was properly recorded as a note receivable by Spaedy Company. You are unsure of how to classify this note on the 20×8 ending balance sheet and ask the president when the note is due. She replies, "We never really set a due date; I might repay it in 20×9 or maybe in a couple of years when I get more financially secure. It would be best to classify this note as a current asset in the usual manner because that will increase our working capital and current ratio, which will make our creditors and stockholders happy."

(Source: Bazley Nikolai Jones. Intermediate Accounting. 余恕莲改编，高等教育出版社，2016.)

From financial reporting and ethical perspectives, what do you think of the president's suggestion?

CHAPTER 7 The Framework of Accounting Principles 会计准则的框架

本章学习目标

1. 理解会计理论中一些重要概念的内涵。
2. 掌握会计假设、会计信息质量特征的基本内容。
3. 理解和掌握采用权责发生制确认收入与费用的基本方法。

本章核心术语

conservatism principle 谨慎性原则
consistency principle 一致性原则
full disclosure principle 充分披露原则
going concern assumption 持续经营假设
matching principle 配比原则
materiality principle 重要性原则
qualitative characteristics 质量特征
realization principle 实现原则
separate entity assumption 会计主体假设
stable monetary unit assumption 货币计量假设

You have learned how accounting procedures are used to properly record business transactions in a sole proprietorship. You also learned how to prepare an income statement, a statement of owner's equity, and a balance sheet to reflect the net income or net loss of a business and to show its financial condition. These accounting procedures and financial statements are based on accounting principles and rules that have come to be generally accepted by the preparers and users of financial information.

7.1 Qualitative Characteristics of Financial Reports 财务报告的质量特征

Qualitative characteristics are qualitative criteria which are used to evaluate the possible measurement options and choose the most appropriate accounting policies for the given situation.

> **知识点解析：**
> qualitative characteristics of financial reports 财务报告的质量特征，是指企业所提供的会计信息的质量标准，其表现为会计信息对于信息使用者决策有用应具备的基本特征，也称为“会计信息质量要求”。

7.1.1 Usefulness

Financial information must be useful to statement readers; otherwise, there is no reason to include it. Usefulness is a rather broad and all-inclusive term and embraces most of the other qualitative characteristics described here.

7.1.2 Relevance

The information shown in the statements must be appropriate for, and have a bearing on, decisions to be made by users of that information.

> **知识点解析：**
> relevance 相关性。相关性是衡量会计信息质量的一项重要指标，指会计信息应与使用者的决策需求相关，即人们可以利用会计信息做出有关的经济决策。如果会计信息能够帮助财务报表使用者评估过去、现在或将来的事件而影响到使用者的决策，那么这种财务信息就具有相关性。信息的相关性包含及时性（timeliness）、预测价值（predictive value）和反馈价值（feedback value）。

7.1.3 Reliability

The information shown in the statements must be dependable, that is, free from error and also free from any bias on the part of the preparer.

知识点解析:

reliability 可靠性。可靠性指会计信息的可信赖程度，是一项重要的信息质量特征。可靠的会计信息必须具备反映真实性（truthfulness）；具有专业资格的不同人员处理同一经济业务应能得到相同的结果，即可验证性（verifiability）；提供信息者必须保持中立的立场进行客观地反映，即中立性（neutrality）。

7.1.4 Understandability

The information must be presented in a manner that is clear and understandable by readers. However, in preparing financial statements, it is assumed that users have a basic knowledge of business and economics and that they will devote an appropriate amount of time to studying and analyzing the statements.

知识点解析:

understandability 可理解性。可理解性指会计所使用的概念和名词，及财务报表的列报必须让报表使用者容易理解。当然，报表使用者本身应当具备一定的会计专业知识，以便透彻地理解财务报表。

7.1.5 Timeliness

Financial information covering an accounting period must be presented quickly enough to be useful in making related decisions.

7.1.6 Comparability

The financial statements for a company must be prepared on a basis that permits comparison with the financial statements of other firms and also with similar data of the company for other periods.

知识点解析：

comparability 可比性。可比性指不同企业提供的财务报表、企业在不同期间提供的财务报表应当具有可比性。因此，要求不同企业在处理同类经济业务时要遵循相同的会计准则，即具有统一性（uniformity）；一个企业所选用的会计政策和程序应在各个会计期间连续使用，即保持一贯性（consistency），除非有合理的原因支持变更。

7.1.7 Completeness

Financial statements are considered complete if all information that would have a material impact on the decisions of users is presented. The key word in this requirement is "material" since financial statements cannot include every item of information about a company because the cost would be prohibitive and some of the data would not be relevant.

7.2 Underlying Assumptions 基本假设

In applying the present body of accounting theory, accountants have used several assumptions about the economy, business enterprises and business activities that make accounting principles meaningful. We will refer to these assumptions as (1) the separate entity assumption, (2) the going concern assumption, (3) the stable monetary unit assumption, and (4) the accounting-period assumption.

7.2.1 Separate Entity Assumption

Accounting records are kept for a particular business organization. The **separate entity** concept assumes that the firm is separate from other businesses and even separate from its owners and creditors. Transactions are recorded in relation to their effects on the business entity. Financial statements summarize these effects for owners, managers, and others. The accounting equation (Assets equal Liabilities plus owner's Equity) expresses the concept concisely.

It is easy to understand the difference between the business entity and its owners in the case of a corporation such as General Motors because the accounting concept of separation agrees with the legal facts. However, the separate entity concept in accounting applies equally to a sole proprietorship or a partnership, even though owners of these types of businesses are legally liable for all debts of the business and for actions carried out on behalf of the business.

知识点解析：

separate entity assumption 会计主体假设。会计主体假设明确了会计核算的空间范围，即将其看作一个独立的经济主体，会计核算是从该经济主体的角度进行的。会计主体的核算要与其所有者个人的经济活动分开，当然，也要与其他的经济主体的交易或事项区分开来。

7.2.2 Going Concern Assumption

When periodic financial reports are prepared for a business, it is generally assumed that the firm is a **going concern** and will continue to operate indefinitely. This assumption permits carrying forward a portion of the cost of assets that will be used in future periods or recognizing revenue that will be earned in the future.

知识点解析：

going concern assumption 持续经营假设。指假定企业在可预见的未来是一个继续存在的实体，其经营活动将会按当前的规模和状态继续经营下去，即能够持续营业，不会大规模削减业务，不会停业，不会面临破产清算，除非有显见或确凿的证据表明其将要倒闭。财务报表的编制基础都是建立在持续经营的前提下的，如果不能满足持续经营的条件，就要改用清算制（即可以卖掉多少钱）的原则去编制。

7.2.3 Stable Monetary Unit Assumption

According records are kept in terms of money, or a stable monetary unit. It is convenient for accountants to assume that the value of money is stable or that changes in its value are not great enough to affect the recorded financial data. The costs of assets purchased many years ago are therefore added to the costs of assets recently purchased, and a total dollar amount is reported.

知识点解析：

stable monetary unit assumption 货币计量假设。指假定货币可以作为一个稳定的计量单位来记录企业的经营活动。该会计假设在实践中也会产生争议性问题，因为它假设货币本身的价值像其他度量单位一样保持稳定不变，但实际情况并非如此。在持续通货膨胀的情况下，会计上必须采取一些措施来弥补该假设的不足。再一个问题就是，企业的一些重要事项将因为无法以货币计量而被排除在财务报表之外，这是不利于决策的，通过财务报表附注提供非财务信息可以在一定程度上弥补这一不足。

7. 2. 4 Accounting-period Assumption

This assumption is contemporary accounting practice to measure the result of an entity's operation over a relatively short period and to present a balance sheet at frequent interval.

The economic activity of a business is continuous. The operating results of any business enterprise cannot be known with certainty until the company has completed its life span and ceased doing business. In the meantime, external decision-makers require timely accounting information to satisfy their analytical needs. To meet their needs, the accounting period assumption requires that changes in a business's financial position be reported over a series of shorter time periods. Some companies use a calendar year, and others use a fiscal year-end that coincides with the low point in business activity over a 12 – month period.

The accounting period assumption does, however, lead to difficulties, First, it should be realized that the shorter the reporting period, the greater the need for estimates and judgment. Over a short period, fewer transactions will be completed and there will be more accruals and deferrals than for longer period. In addition, financial reports for short periods may provide misleading impressions of the long-run prospects for the firm. A balance sheet represents a "snap-shot" of the entity's financial position at an instant of time. Immediately before and after the date of the balance sheet, the financial position is different.

知识点解析：

accounting-period assumption 会计分期假设。即根据持续经营假设，将不断循环的经营过程划分为较短的时间段落，在每一个段落结束时，进行一次结算，确定这一期间的盈亏。这种分段计算盈亏的时间区间，称为会计期间（accounting period），也称作 fiscal period。为期 12 个月的会计期间为一个会计年度，会计年度可以与日历年度一致，也可以不一致，有些国家允许企业根据自身的生产经营特点确定其会计年度。

7. 3 General Principles 一般原则

In deciding how a transaction should be recorded and how its effects should be reported on the financial statements, accountants must keep in mind several basic accounting principles or concepts that serve as guides.

7.3.1 Cost Basis Principle

Business transactions are, almost without exception, recorded on a **cost basis**, which is the amount of money determined through dealings in the market between the business and outsiders. Assets are carried at cost until they are used. At that time the cost (or an appropriate part of it) is charged against revenue. Cost is preferred to some possible alternatives, such as appraisal value, because cost, when determined in an "arm's length" transaction (a transaction with outsiders), is an objective, verifiable measure of economic value.

知识点解析:

"arm's length" transactions 正常交易。在公平市价基础上所做的正常交易，买卖双方在不受任何影响和约束，各自寻求其本身的经济利益的情况下议定出交易价格，称为正常交易。与其相对的情况是个人关系交易（arm-in-arm transaction），即在交易中加入了个人关系，交易价格也就很可能不是公平价格。

7.3.2 Realization Principle

Since accounting reports focus on the measurement of income for the fiscal period, one critical problem is the determination of the period in which to record revenue and to report it on the income statement. Revenue represents the inflow of new assets resulting from the sale of goods or services. Thus, as a general rule, revenue is recognized when a sale is made or a service is provided to an outsider. The **realization** of revenue occurs at the time new assets are created in the form of money or in claims against others. Thus accountant usually say that revenue should not be recognized until it has been realized.

7.3.3 Principle of Matching Costs with Revenue

If income is to be properly measured, revenues must be matched against the expired costs incurred in earning those revenues. This concept is referred to as the **matching principle**. To achieve matching, the accountant seeks systematic, rational approaches for determining the period in which costs should be charged against revenues.

Some costs, such as manufacturing costs, can easily be identified with specific products. It is customary to treat these costs as inventory costs and to charge them to cost of goods sold when the products are sold. Other costs, such as office salaries, do not clearly benefit future periods and are charged as expenses when they are incurred. Still other costs benefit many future periods. The accountant therefore seeks to estimate the periods benefited and to charge the costs as expenses during the periods involved. For example, the cost of a store building is depreciated over its estimated useful life.

Many of the controversial questions in accounting involve determining the period or periods in which a cost should be charged as an expense.

知识点解析：

matching principle 配比原则，又称配合原则。这是指导费用确认的会计原则，指将企业一个时期的收入和费用依据权责发生制相配比，按照收入与费用的因果关系或收入与产生收入所耗用费用的期间相配比，以确定企业的经营成果。

例如，通过确认当期销售收入，并结转当期销售成本，以此计算当期销售毛利；计算当期净利润时要将当期实现的所有收入配比当期发生的所有费用。但在物价不断上涨的情况下，以历史成本和现实收入相配比就不能向会计报表使用者提供真实可靠的会计信息。

7.3.4 Accrual Principle

Inherent in the realization principle and the matching principle is the **accrual principle**, which you learned about in earlier chapters. Sometimes a transaction occurs in one period but the cash involved is not received or paid out until a later period. Under the accrual principle, transactions are recorded in the period in which they occur, rather than in the period when the cash inflow or outflow takes place.

知识点解析：

accrual principle，即 accrual basis of accounting 权责发生制，也称应计制。即根据收入的赚得和费用的发生来确认收入和费用，而不论是否收到或付出现金。权责发生制体现了收入实现原则、配比原则和会计期间假设，可恰当反映一个期间的经营成果。

与权责发生制相对的是收付实现制（cash basis of accounting）。即在收到现金时确认收入，在付出现金时确认费用，不考虑收入与费用所应归属的期间。由于它忽略了已经赚得但尚未收到的收入和已经发生但尚未付出的费用，因而不能正确反映收益的实现情况。

For example, suppose that employees work in December but are not paid until January of the following year. Their earnings should be recorded as an expense in December, and the amount owed to them at the end of December should be shown as a liability on the December 31 balance sheet. Similarly, if a firm purchases office supplies in December and uses only a portion of them in that month, the cost should be allocated so that the part used is treated as an expense and the part still on hand is reported as an asset.

Test your understanding

Which of the following statements is true?

A. The accrual basis of accounting matches revenue earned with expenses paid

B. The cash basis of accounting matches revenue received with expenses incurred

C. The accrual basis of accounting matches revenue received with expenses paid

D. The cash basis of accounting matches revenue received with expenses paid

7.3.5 Consistency Principle

The **consistency principle** requires that the application of a given accounting procedure be the same from one period to the next in a particular company. Any lack of consistency would result in financial reports that are not comparable with earlier reports and are therefore misleading.

However, the consistency rule does not mean that no changes in accounting principles or methods can be made. If the application of another accounting method would clearly give a fairer presentation of earnings or financial position, it is proper to change to the new method. Detailed rules have been developed for reporting the effects of the change so that statement users are completely informed.

知识点解析：

consistency principle 一致性原则。即在不同会计期间所使用的会计程序和会计方法应保持一致，但会计程序和方法并非永远不能变动，如果发生了重要的变动，必须在财务报表的附注中加以说明。

7.3.6 Full Disclosure Principle

Full disclosure requires that all information that might affect the statement user's interpretation of the profitability and financial position of a business must be disclosed in the business's financial statements or in footnotes to the statements. In recent years there have been numerous lawsuits by statement users against certified public accountants and against companies issuing financial statements. The lawsuits have charged that the statements of these companies did not disclose facts that would have influenced investor decisions. As a result, accountants are careful to include enough information so that the informed reader can obtain a complete and accurate picture. The financial reports issued by large companies usually include a thorough explanation of the accounting principles and methods that have been used in preparing the statements.

7.4 Modifying Conventions 修正性的惯例

Although the basic accounting principles and underlying assumptions provide a means for analyzing each business transaction to determine its proper treatment in the accounts, a number of practical considerations have come to be accepted as limiting or modifying the application of the general principles. Among the most important of these modifying conventions are materiality, conservatism and substance over form.

知识点解析:

accounting convention 会计惯例。会计惯例指在长期的会计实践中形成的为大家所接受的概念、方法和程序。在西方的会计资料中有时并不严格区分假设、惯例、原则、概念等术语，因此该术语有时可与 principle、concept、assumption 通用。

7.4.1 Materiality

Materiality concerns the significance of an item in relation to the particular situation of which it is a part. An item of a certain dollar amount might be material in a small company and thus would have to be disclosed. However, the same amount might not be significant in a larger firm and could therefore be combined with other figures or be presented in a different manner on the statements.

Although no hard-and-fast rules for judging materiality have been laid down, an item is usually compared with the firm's net income and with total owner's equity in deciding whether it is material. It is generally accepted that a deviation from normal accounting principles is permissible if the amount is immaterial. For example, a business that has sales of ¥10 million a year might buy a small tool with a useful life of three years for ￥50. Practicality dictates that this item be charged as an expense rather than recorded as an asset and then depreciated over its useful life. The amount of this transaction is immaterial in such a large business. Although this example is extreme, it indicates the concept involved.

知识点解析：

materiality 重要性。即对金额不大或对决策影响不大的交易和事项，可以不在财务报表或附注中予以单独反映，而财务报表对重大或重要事项未作披露就很可能会使信息使用者做出错误决策。一个交易或事项是否重要，既取决于其金额，也取决于其性质，因此，重要性原则的运用有一定的主观性，需要会计人员的职业判断(professional judgement)。同时，重要性也是一个审计领域中的专有名词。

7.4.2 Conservatism

Accountants have long followed a doctrine of **conservatism**, under which assets are understated rather than overstated if any question exists. Recognition of income is deferred until it is realized, and losses and expenses are recognized as soon as they occur.

Although this convention is still basically accepted by most accountants, an increasing number concede that undue conservatism in the present may make for a lack of conservatism in the future. For example, if too much of the cost of an asset is charged as depreciation expense in the present period, the firm's net income will be conservatively reported and the book value of the asset will be conservatively stated. In later years, during which the asset still performs useful service, the depreciation expense will be understated and the net income will be correspondingly overstated, which is not conservative. Increased accuracy of valuation and timing has come to be more important to many accountants than the old-style conservatism.

知识点解析：

conservatism 谨慎性。谨慎性表现的是一种合理的保守主义，该原则要求在经济业务或事项存在不确定性的情况下，通常确认全部的费用和可能发生的损失，但不确认任何可能的收入或利得，从而使财务报表所提供的财务状况和经营成果是最保守的结果，避免引起管理层的过分乐观。

7.4.3 Substance over Form

Faithful representation of a transaction is only possible if it is accounted for according to its substance and economic reality.

Substance over form principle requires that transactions and other events are accounted for and presented in accordance with their substance and economic reality and not merely their legal form. In other words, accounting information should represent what it purports to represent and should report the economic substance of transactions, not just their form or surface appearance. Substance over form usually applies to transactions which are fairly complicated. It is very important because it acts as a far-reaching principle to stop enterprises distorting their results by following the letter of the law, instead of showing what the enterprise has really been doing.

知识点解析：

substance over form 实质重于形式。即要求企业以交易或事项的经济实质进行会计确认、计量和报告，不仅仅以交易或事项的法律形式为依据。在多数情况下，企业发生的交易或事项的经济实质和法律形式是一致的，但在有些情况下也会出现不一致。

例如，企业按照销售合同销售商品但又签订了售后回购协议，从经济实质上看并没有将商品所有权上的主要风险和报酬转移给购货方，即使在法律形式上签订了商品销售合同或已经将商品交付给购货方，也不应当确认销售收入。又如，融资租赁业务的会计处理遵循了实质重于形式原则，合并报表也是按经济实质而不是法律形式来反映母公司对子公司的控股关系及其事实结果的。

For example, business may have entered into a leasing agreement for some equipment. However, the terms are such that the business is really buying the equipment. The equipment should be included in the statement of financial position and the leasing agreement should be treated as a financing arrangement.

Test your understanding

Which of the following statements about accounting concepts are correct?

A. The money measurement concepts is that only items capable of being measured in monetary terms can be recognised in financial statements

B. The prudence concept means that understating of assets and overstating of liabilities is desirable in preparing financial statements

C. The historical cost concept is that assets are initially recognised at their transaction cost

D. The substance over form convention is that, whenever legally possible, the economic substance of a transaction should be reflected in financial statements rather than simply its legal form

Test your understanding

Which of the following statements best explains the principle of faithful representation in relation preparation of the annual financial statements?

A. Transactions are presented any way that is considered appropriate

B. Transactions are presented in such a way as to maximise profit for the year

C. Transactions are presented in such a way to maximise asset values in the statement of financial position

D. Transactions are presented to reflect their commercial substance of a transaction rather than their legal form

本章小结：

会计基本概念与原则是指导会计实务工作、确保会计系统高效运行的理论基础。我们将一些重要的会计概念与原则分为四类：质量特征、基本假设、基本原则和修正性的惯例。财务报告的质量特征包括有用性、相关性、可靠性、可理解性、及时性、可比性和完整性。基本假设包括会计主体假设、持续经营假设、货币计量假设和会计分期假设。会计基本原则包括：历史成本原则、实现原则、配比原则、应计制原则、一致性原则、充分披露原则。修正性的惯例包括：重要性、谨慎性、实质重于形式。

Self – Review & Questions 自测题

1. What does accounting-period assumption mean? What problems in accounting perspective does it cause?

2. What does matching principle mean? Why is it important to income measurement?

3. Explain conservatism. Why did it become an accounting convention?

4. Explain what is meant by the cost basis of accounting.

5. How do accountants use the concept of materiality?

6. What does substance over form mean? Why is it important?

7. What does separate entity assumption imply to accounting? How to identify an accounting entity?

8. What are the advantages of accrual basis of accounting?

Translations 翻译题

Translate the following English into Chinese or Chinese into English.

1. Users of financial reports have a right to expect that the statements are objective—that they are unbiased and fair to all parties. In addition, users are entitled to assume that the statements are based on verifiable evidence rather than on opinions.

2. Often businesses encounter new or unusual transactions that give rise to accounting questions that do not appear to have simple solutions. Thus an understanding of the accounting concepts is essential to an understanding of complex accounting issues.

3. Financial statements are of great importance in managerial decision making. Thus management should understand the basic principles that underlie financial statements.

4. The information allows management to evaluate the results of operations and the financial position of the business and to make decisions.

5. Creditors, prospective investors, governmental agencies, and many others are also vitally interested in the profits of the business and in the asset and equity structure.

6. 解读财务数据是会计的一项重要职能，会计也常被称为一门艺术。

7. 权责发生制比收付实现制更能合理地反映企业的经营业绩，同时也能增强各期间会计信息的可比性。

8. 我们经常需要对不同的信息质量特征进行权衡，特别是相关性和可靠性。可靠性可能会随着相关性的增加而减弱，反之亦然。

Exercises 练习题

Select the best answer for each of the following items.

1. A profit-making business operating as a separate legal entity and in which ownership is divided into shares of stock is known as a (   ).

A. proprietorship　　B. service business

C. partnership　　D. corporation

2. The resources owned by a business are called (   ).

A. assets　　B. liabilities

C. the accounting equation　　D. owner's equity

3. A listing of a business entity's assets, liabilities, and owner's equity as of a specific date is (   ).

A. a balance sheet B. an income statement

C. the statement of owner's equity D. a statement of cash flows

4. If revenue was ¥45 000, expenses were ¥37 500, and dividends were ¥10 000, the amount of net income or net loss would be ( ).

A. ¥45 000 net income B. ¥7 500 net income

C. ¥37 500 net loss D. ¥2 500 net loss

5. The purchase of land for ¥50 000 cash was incorrectly recorded as an increase in land and an increase in notes payable. Which of the following statements is correct? ( )

A. The accounting equation will not balance because cash is overstated by ¥50 000

B. The accounting equation will not balance because notes payable are overstated by ¥50 000

C. The accounting equation will not balance because assets will exceed liabilities by ¥50 000

D. Even though a recording error has been made, the accounting equation will balance

6. The receipt of ¥8 000 cash for fees income was recorded as an increase in cash of ¥8 000 and a decrease in revenue of ¥8 000. What is the effect of this error on the accounting equation? ( )

A. Total assets will exceed total liabilities and owner's equity by ¥8 000

B. Total assets will be less than total liabilities and owner's equity by ¥8 000

C. Total assets will exceed total liabilities and owner's equity ¥16 000

D. The error will not affect the accounting equation

7. If total assets increased ¥20 000 during a period and total liabilities increased ¥12 000 during the same period, the amount and direction (increase or decrease) of the change in owner's equity for that period is ( ).

A. a ¥32 000 increase B. a ¥32 000 decrease

C. an ¥8 000 increase D. an ¥8 000 decrease

8. Which of the following transactions changes assets and does not affect liabilities or owner's equity? ( )

A. Borrowed ¥40 000 from First National Bank

B. Purchased land for cash

C. Received ¥3 800 for fees earned

D. Paid ¥4 000 for office salaries

9. Assume that a lawyer bills her clients ¥15 000 on June 30, 20×8, for services rendered during June. The lawyer collects ¥8 500 during July and the remainder in August. Under the accrual basis of accounting, when would the lawyer record the revenue for the fees? ( )

A. June, ¥15 000; July, ¥0; and August, ¥0

B. June, ¥0; July, ¥6 500; and August, ¥8 500

C. June, ¥8 500; July, ¥6 500; and August, ¥0

D. June, ¥0; July, ¥8 500; and August, ¥6 500

10. On January 24, 20×8, ABC Co. collected ¥5 700 it had billed its clients for services rendered on December 31, 20×7. How would you record the January 24 transaction, using the accrual basis? ( )

A. Increase Cash, ¥5 700; decrease Fees Income, ¥5 700

B. Increase Accounts Receivable, ¥5 700; increase Fees Income, ¥5 700

C. Increase Cash, ¥5 700; decrease Accounts Receivable, ¥5 700

D. Increase Cash, ¥5 700; increase Fees Income, ¥5 700

11. Which of the following items represents a deferral? ( )

A. Prepaid insurance B. Wages payable

C. Fees earned D. Accumulated depreciation

12. If the supplies account indicated a balance of ¥2 250 before adjustment on May 31 and supplies on hand at May 31 totaled ¥950, the adjustment would be ( ).

A. increase Supplies, ¥950; decrease Supplies Expense, ¥950

B. increase Supplies, ¥1 300; decrease Supplies Expense, ¥1 300

C. increase Supplies Expense, ¥950; decrease Supplies, ¥950

D. increase Supplies Expense, ¥1 300; decrease Supplies, ¥1 300

13. The balance in the unearned rent account for ABC Co. as of December 31 is ¥1 200. If ABC Co. failed to record the adjusting entry for ¥600 of rent earned during December, the effect on the balance sheet and income statement for December would be ( ).

A. assets understated by ¥600; net income overstated by ¥600

B. liabilities understated by ¥600; net income understated by ¥600

C. liabilities overstated by ¥600; net income understated by ¥600

D. liabilities overstated by ¥600; net income overstated by ¥600

Case Analysis 案例分析

It is the end of 20×7, and, as an accountant for Newell Company, you are preparing its 20×7 financial statements. On December 29, 20×7, the management of Newell decided to sell one of its major divisions, subject to some legal work that is expected to be completed during the first week in April 20×8 (after the 20×7 financial statements have been issued). During 20×7, the division earned a small operating income that is just enough for the company to report "record earnings" for the year. However, the estimated fair value of the division at the end of 20×7 is less than its net book value, so that management anticipates the component will be sold at a loss.

The president of Newell stops by your office and says to you, "You have been doing a fine job. Keep up the good work, because you are heading for a promotion in early 20×9. Once we report the record earnings for 20×7, our stockholders and creditors will be happy. Then I think our earnings for 20×8 will be high enough so that the loss we expect to report in 20×8 on the sale of the division will not look so bad." After the president leaves your office, you continue preparing the 20×7 financial statements.

(Source: Bazley Nikolai Jones. Intermediate Accounting. 余恕莲改编，高等教育出版社，2016.)

Form financial reporting and ethical perspectives, what information, if any, will you include about the upcoming sale of the division in the 20×7 financial statements?

附录1　企业会计准则——基本准则

2006年2月，我国会计准则发布，在发布的基本准则中，建立了与IASB概念框架类似的概念体系。为了适应我国企业和资本市场发展的实际需要，实现我国企业会计准则与国际财务报告准则的持续趋同，2014年7月，根据《财政部关于修改〈企业会计准则——基本准则〉的决定》公布了修改后的基本准则。以下为修改后的《企业会计准则——基本准则》全文。

第一章　总则

第一条　为了规范企业会计确认、计量和报告行为，保证会计信息质量，根据《中华人民共和国会计法》和其他有关法律、行政法规，制定本准则。

第二条　本准则适用于在中华人民共和国境内设立的企业（包括公司，下同）。

第三条　企业会计准则包括基本准则和具体准则，具体准则的制定应当遵循本准则。

第四条　企业应当编制财务会计报告（又称财务报告，下同）。财务会计报告的目标是向财务会计报告使用者提供与企业财务状况、经营成果和现金流量等有关的会计信息，反映企业管理层受托责任履行情况，有助于财务会计报告使用者作出经济决策。

财务会计报告使用者包括投资者、债权人、政府及其有关部门和社会公众等。

第五条　企业应当对其本身发生的交易或者事项进行会计确认、计量和报告。

第六条　企业会计确认、计量和报告应当以持续经营为前提。

第七条　企业应当划分会计期间，分期结算账目和编制财务会计报告。

会计期间分为年度和中期。中期是指短于一个完整的会计年度的报告期间。

第八条　企业会计应当以货币计量。

第九条　企业应当以权责发生制为基础进行会计确认、计量和报告。

第十条　企业应当按照交易或者事项的经济特征确定会计要素。会计要素包括资产、负债、所有者权益、收入、费用和利润。

第十一条　企业应当采用借贷记账法记账。

第二章　会计信息质量要求

第十二条　企业应当以实际发生的交易或者事项为依据进行会计确认、计量和报告，如实反映符合确认和计量要求的各项会计要素及其他相关信息，保证会计信息真实可靠、内容完整。

第十三条　企业提供的会计信息应当与财务会计报告使用者的经济决策需要相关，有助于财务会计报告使用者对企业过去、现在或者未来的情况作出评价或者预测。

第十四条　企业提供的会计信息应当清晰明了，便于财务会计报告使用者理解和使用。

第十五条　企业提供的会计信息应当具有可比性。

同一企业不同时期发生的相同或者相似的交易或者事项，应当采用一致的会计政策，不得随意变更。确需变更的，应当在附注中说明。

不同企业发生的相同或者相似的交易或者事项，应当采用规定的会计政策，确保会计信息口径一致、相互可比。

第十六条　企业应当按照交易或者事项的经济实质进行会计确认、计量和报告，不应仅以交易或者事项的法律形式为依据。

第十七条　企业提供的会计信息应当反映与企业财务状况、经营成果和现金流量等有关的所有重要交易或者事项。

第十八条　企业对交易或者事项进行会计确认、计量和报告应当保持应有的谨慎，不应高估资产或者收益、低估负债或者费用。

第十九条　企业对于已经发生的交易或者事项，应当及时进行会计确认、计量和报告，不得提前或者延后。

第三章　资产

第二十条　资产是指企业过去的交易或者事项形成的、由企业拥有或者控制的、预期会给企业带来经济利益的资源。

前款所指的企业过去的交易或者事项包括购买、生产、建造行为或其他交易或者事项。预期在未来发生的交易或者事项不形成资产。

由企业拥有或者控制，是指企业享有某项资源的所有权，或者虽然不享有某项资源的所有权，但该资源能被企业所控制。

预期会给企业带来经济利益，是指直接或者间接导致现金和现金等价物流入企业的潜力。

第二十一条　符合本准则第二十条规定的资产定义的资源，在同时满足以下条件时，确认为资产：

（一）与该资源有关的经济利益很可能流入企业；

（二）该资源的成本或者价值能够可靠地计量。

第二十二条　符合资产定义和资产确认条件的项目，应当列入资产负债表；符合资产定义、但不符合资产确认条件的项目，不应当列入资产负债表。

第四章　负债

第二十三条　负债是指企业过去的交易或者事项形成的、预期会导致经济利益流出企业的现时义务。

现时义务是指企业在现行条件下已承担的义务。未来发生的交易或者事项形成的义务，不属于现时义务，不应当确认为负债。

第二十四条　符合本准则第二十三条规定的负债定义的义务，在同时满足以下条件时，确认为负债：

（一）与该义务有关的经济利益很可能流出企业；

（二）未来流出的经济利益的金额能够可靠地计量。

第二十五条　符合负债定义和负债确认条件的项目，应当列入资产负债表；符合负债定义、但不符合负债确认条件的项目，不应当列入资产负债表。

第五章　所有者权益

第二十六条　所有者权益是指企业资产扣除负债后由所有者享有的剩余权益。

公司的所有者权益又称为股东权益。

第二十七条　所有者权益的来源包括所有者投入的资本、直接计入所有者权益的利得和损失、留存收益等。

直接计入所有者权益的利得和损失，是指不应计入当期损益、会导致所有者权益发生增减变动的、与所有者投入资本或者向所有者分配利润无关的利得或者损失。

利得是指由企业非日常活动所形成的、会导致所有者权益增加的、与所有者投入资本无关的经济利益的流入。

损失是指由企业非日常活动所发生的、会导致所有者权益减少的、与向所有者分配利润无关的经济利益的流出。

第二十八条　所有者权益金额取决于资产和负债的计量。

第二十九条　所有者权益项目应当列入资产负债表。

第六章　收入

第三十条　收入是指企业在日常活动中形成的、会导致所有者权益增加的、与所有者投入资本无关的经济利益的总流入。

第三十一条　收入只有在经济利益很可能流入从而导致企业资产增加或者负债减少、且经济利益的流入额能够可靠计量时才能予以确认。

第三十二条　符合收入定义和收入确认条件的项目，应当列入利润表。

第七章　费用

第三十三条　费用是指企业在日常活动中发生的、会导致所有者权益减少的、与向所有者分配利润无关的经济利益的总流出。

第三十四条　费用只有在经济利益很可能流出从而导致企业资产减少或者负债增加、且经济利益的流出额能够可靠计量时才能予以确认。

第三十五条　企业为生产产品、提供劳务等发生的可归属于产品成本、劳务成本等的费用，应当在确认产品销售收入、劳务收入等时，将已销售产品、已提供劳务的成本等计入当期损益。

企业发生的支出不产生经济利益的，或者即使能够产生经济利益但不符合或者不再符合资产确认条件的，应当在发生时确认为费用，计入当期损益。

企业发生的交易或者事项导致其承担了一项负债而又不确认为一项资产的，应当在发生时确认为费用，计入当期损益。

第三十六条　符合费用定义和费用确认条件的项目，应当列入利润表。

第八章　利润

第三十七条　利润是指企业在一定会计期间的经营成果。利润包括收入减去费用后的净额、直接计入当期利润的利得和损失等。

第三十八条　直接计入当期利润的利得和损失，是指应当计入当期损益、会导致所有者权益发生增减变动的、与所有者投入资本或者向所有者分配利润无关的利得或者损失。

第三十九条　利润金额取决于收入和费用、直接计入当期利润的利得和损失金额的计量。

第四十条　利润项目应当列入利润表。

第九章　会计计量

第四十一条　企业在将符合确认条件的会计要素登记入账并列报于会计报表及其附注（又称财务报表，下同）时，应当按照规定的会计计量属性进行计量，确定其金额。

第四十二条　会计计量属性主要包括：

（一）历史成本。在历史成本计量下，资产按照购置时支付的现金或者现金等价物的金额，或者按照购置资产时所付出的对价的公允价值计量。负债按照因承担现时义务而实际收到的款项或者资产的金额，或者承担现时义务的合同金额，或者按照日常活动中为偿还负债预期需要支付的现金或者现金等价物的金额计量。

（二）重置成本。在重置成本计量下，资产按照现在购买相同或者相似资产所需支付的现金或者现金等价物的金额计量。负债按照现在偿付该项债务所需支付的现金或者现金等价物的金额计量。

（三）可变现净值。在可变现净值计量下，资产按照其正常对外销售所能收到现金或者现金等价物的金额扣减该资产至完工时估计将要发生的成本、估计的销售费用以及相关税费后的金额计量。

（四）现值。在现值计量下，资产按照预计从其持续使用和最终处置中所产生的未来净现金流入量的折现金额计量。负债按照预计期限内需要偿还的未来净现金流出量的折现金额计量。

（五）公允价值。在公允价值计量下，资产和负债按照市场参与者在计量日发生的有序交易中，出售资产所能收到或者转移负债所需支付的价格计量。

第四十三条　企业在对会计要素进行计量时，一般应当采用历史成本，采用重置成本、可变现净值、现值、公允价值计量的，应当保证所确定的会计要素金额能够取得并可靠计量。

第十章　财务会计报告

第四十四条　财务会计报告是指企业对外提供的反映企业某一特定日期的财务状况和某一会计期间的经营成果、现金流量等会计信息的文件。

财务会计报告包括会计报表及其附注和其他应当在财务会计报告中披露的相关信息

和资料。会计报表至少应当包括资产负债表、利润表、现金流量表等报表。

小企业编制的会计报表可以不包括现金流量表。

第四十五条 资产负债表是指反映企业在某一特定日期的财务状况的会计报表。

第四十六条 利润表是指反映企业在一定会计期间的经营成果的会计报表。

第四十七条 现金流量表是指反映企业在一定会计期间的现金和现金等价物流入和流出的会计报表。

第四十八条 附注是指对在会计报表中列示项目所作的进一步说明，以及对未能在这些报表中列示项目的说明等。

资料来源：http：//tfs. mof. gov. cn/zhengwuxinxi/caizhengbuling/201407/t20140729_1119494. html。

附录 2　管理会计基本指引

管理会计是社会生产力进步、管理水平提高的结果，也是一门有助于提高经济效益的科学。在西方的企业中，会计机构隶属于支持生产部门工作并为其服务的服务部门，管理会计、财务会计分别有专职的人员，两个基本部门并行，共同接受总会计师的领导。如今，财务会计工作面对人工智能的挑战，转型升级已是当务之急，发展管理会计已经成为大势所趋。

2016 年 6 月，财政部根据《中华人民共和国会计法》《财政部关于全面推进管理会计体系建设的指导意见》等，制定了《管理会计基本指引》，为我国单位企业和行政事业单位全面准确理解管理会计、科学系统应用管理会计提供了基本框架和方向。以下为《管理会计基本指引》全文。

第一章　总则

第一条　为促进单位（包括企业和行政事业单位，下同）加强管理会计工作，提升内部管理水平，促进经济转型升级，根据《中华人民共和国会计法》《财政部关于全面推进管理会计体系建设的指导意见》等，制定本指引。

第二条　基本指引在管理会计指引体系中起统领作用，是制定应用指引和建设案例库的基础。管理会计指引体系包括基本指引、应用指引和案例库，用以指导单位管理会计实践。

第三条　管理会计的目标是通过运用管理会计工具方法，参与单位规划、决策、控制、评价活动并为之提供有用信息，推动单位实现战略规划。

第四条　单位应用管理会计，应遵循下列原则：

（一）战略导向原则。管理会计的应用应以战略规划为导向，以持续创造价值为核心，促进单位可持续发展。

（二）融合性原则。管理会计应嵌入单位相关领域、层次、环节，以业务流程为基础，利用管理会计工具方法，将财务和业务等有机融合。

（三）适应性原则。管理会计的应用应与单位应用环境和自身特征相适应。单位自身特征包括单位性质、规模、发展阶段、管理模式、治理水平等。

（四）成本效益原则。管理会计的应用应权衡实施成本和预期效益，合理、有效地推进管理会计应用。

第五条　管理会计应用主体视管理决策主体确定，可以是单位整体，也可以是单位内部的责任中心。

第六条　单位应用管理会计，应包括应用环境、管理会计活动、工具方法、信息与报告等四要素。

第二章 应用环境

第七条 单位应用管理会计，应充分了解和分析其应用环境。管理会计应用环境，是单位应用管理会计的基础，包括内外部环境。

内部环境主要包括与管理会计建设和实施相关的价值创造模式、组织架构、管理模式、资源保障、信息系统等因素。

外部环境主要包括国内外经济、市场、法律、行业等因素。

第八条 单位应准确分析和把握价值创造模式，推动财务与业务等的有机融合。

第九条 单位应根据组织架构特点，建立健全能够满足管理会计活动所需的由财务、业务等相关人员组成的管理会计组织体系。有条件的单位可以设置管理会计机构，组织开展管理会计工作。

第十条 单位应根据管理模式确定责任主体，明确各层级以及各层级内的部门、岗位之间的管理会计责任权限，制定管理会计实施方案，以落实管理会计责任。

第十一条 单位应从人力、财力、物力等方面做好资源保障工作，加强资源整合，提高资源利用效率效果，确保管理会计工作顺利开展。

单位应注重管理会计理念、知识培训，加强管理会计人才培养。

第十二条 单位应将管理会计信息化需求纳入信息系统规划，通过信息系统整合、改造或新建等途径，及时、高效地提供和管理相关信息，推进管理会计实施。

第三章 管理会计活动

第十三条 管理会计活动是单位利用管理会计信息，运用管理会计工具方法，在规划、决策、控制、评价等方面服务于单位管理需要的相关活动。

第十四条 单位应用管理会计，应做好相关信息支持，参与战略规划拟定，从支持其定位、目标设定、实施方案选择等方面，为单位合理制定战略规划提供支撑。

第十五条 单位应用管理会计，应融合财务和业务等活动，及时充分提供和利用相关信息，支持单位各层级根据战略规划做出决策。

第十六条 单位应用管理会计，应设定定量定性标准，强化分析、沟通、协调、反馈等控制机制，支持和引导单位持续高质高效地实施单位战略规划。

第十七条 单位应用管理会计，应合理设计评价体系，基于管理会计信息等，评价单位战略规划实施情况，并以此为基础进行考核，完善激励机制；同时，对管理会计活动进行评估和完善，以持续改进管理会计应用。

第四章 工具方法

第十八条 管理会计工具方法是实现管理会计目标的具体手段。

第十九条 管理会计工具方法是单位应用管理会计时所采用的战略地图、滚动预算管理、作业成本管理、本量利分析、平衡计分卡等模型、技术、流程的统称。管理会计工具方法具有开放性，随着实践发展不断丰富完善。

第二十条 管理会计工具方法主要应用于以下领域：战略管理、预算管理、成本管理、营运管理、投融资管理、绩效管理、风险管理等。

（一）战略管理领域应用的管理会计工具方法包括但不限于战略地图、价值链管理等；

（二）预算管理领域应用的管理会计工具方法包括但不限于全面预算管理、滚动预算管理、作业预算管理、零基预算管理、弹性预算管理等；

（三）成本管理领域应用的管理会计工具方法包括但不限于目标成本管理、标准成本管理、变动成本管理、作业成本管理、生命周期成本管理等；

（四）营运管理领域应用的管理会计工具方法包括但不限于本量利分析、敏感性分析、边际分析、标杆管理等；

（五）投融资管理领域应用的管理会计工具方法包括但不限于贴现现金流法、项目管理、资本成本分析等；

（六）绩效管理领域应用的管理会计工具方法包括但不限于关键指标法、经济增加值、平衡计分卡等；

（七）风险管理领域应用的管理会计工具方法包括但不限于单位风险管理框架、风险矩阵模型等。

第二十一条　单位应用管理会计，应结合自身实际情况，根据管理特点和实践需要选择适用的管理会计工具方法，并加强管理会计工具方法的系统化、集成化应用。

第五章　信息与报告

第二十二条　管理会计信息包括管理会计应用过程中所使用和生成的财务信息和非财务信息。

第二十三条　单位应充分利用内外部各种渠道，通过采集、转换等多种方式，获得相关、可靠的管理会计基础信息。

第二十四条　单位应有效利用现代信息技术，对管理会计基础信息进行加工、整理、分析和传递，以满足管理会计应用需要。

第二十五条　单位生成的管理会计信息应相关、可靠、及时、可理解。

第二十六条　管理会计报告是管理会计活动成果的重要表现形式，旨在为报告使用者提供满足管理需要的信息。管理会计报告按期间可以分为定期报告和不定期报告，按内容可以分为综合性报告和专项报告等类别。

第二十七条　单位可以根据管理需要和管理会计活动性质设定报告期间。一般应以公历期间作为报告期间，也可以根据特定需要设定报告期间。

资料来源：http：//kjs. mof. gov. cn/zhengwuxinxi/zhengcefabu/201606/t20160624_2336654. html。

附录 3　政府会计准则——基本准则

随着我国政治体制改革不断深入，逐渐对政府会计产生了新的要求。为加快推进政府会计改革，构建统一、科学、规范的政府会计标准体系和权责发生制政府综合财务报告制度，2015 年 10 月，财政部公布了《政府会计准则——基本准则》。《政府会计准则——基本准则》作为政府会计的“概念框架”，统驭政府会计具体准则和政府会计制度的制定，并为政府会计实务问题提供处理原则，为编制政府财务报告提供基础标准。以下为《政府会计准则——基本准则》全文。

第一章　总则

第一条　为了规范政府的会计核算，保证会计信息质量，根据《中华人民共和国会计法》《中华人民共和国预算法》和其他有关法律、行政法规，制定本准则。

第二条　本准则适用于各级政府、各部门、各单位（以下统称政府会计主体）。

前款所称各部门、各单位是指与本级政府财政部门直接或者间接发生预算拨款关系的国家机关、军队、政党组织、社会团体、事业单位和其他单位。

军队、已纳入企业财务管理体系的单位和执行《民间非营利组织会计制度》的社会团体，不适用本准则。

第三条　政府会计由预算会计和财务会计构成。

预算会计实行收付实现制，国务院另有规定的，依照其规定。

财务会计实行权责发生制。

第四条　政府会计具体准则及其应用指南、政府会计制度等，应当由财政部遵循本准则制定。

第五条　政府会计主体应当编制决算报告和财务报告。

决算报告的目标是向决算报告使用者提供与政府预算执行情况有关的信息，综合反映政府会计主体预算收支的年度执行结果，有助于决算报告使用者进行监督和管理，并为编制后续年度预算提供参考和依据。政府决算报告使用者包括各级人民代表大会及其常务委员会、各级政府及其有关部门、政府会计主体自身、社会公众和其他利益相关者。

财务报告的目标是向财务报告使用者提供与政府的财务状况、运行情况（含运行成本，下同）和现金流量等有关信息，反映政府会计主体公共受托责任履行情况，有助于财务报告使用者作出决策或者进行监督和管理。政府财务报告使用者包括各级人民代表大会常务委员会、债权人、各级政府及其有关部门、政府会计主体自身和其他利益相关者。

第六条　政府会计主体应当对其自身发生的经济业务或者事项进行会计核算。

第七条　政府会计核算应当以政府会计主体持续运行为前提。

第八条　政府会计核算应当划分会计期间，分期结算账目，按规定编制决算报告和财务报告。

会计期间至少分为年度和月度。会计年度、月度等会计期间的起讫日期采用公历日期。

第九条　政府会计核算应当以人民币作为记账本位币。发生外币业务时，应当将有关外币金额折算为人民币金额计量，同时登记外币金额。

第十条　政府会计核算应当采用借贷记账法记账。

第二章　政府会计信息质量要求

第十一条　政府会计主体应当以实际发生的经济业务或者事项为依据进行会计核算，如实反映各项会计要素的情况和结果，保证会计信息真实可靠。

第十二条　政府会计主体应当将发生的各项经济业务或者事项统一纳入会计核算，确保会计信息能够全面反映政府会计主体预算执行情况和财务状况、运行情况、现金流量等。

第十三条　政府会计主体提供的会计信息，应当与反映政府会计主体公共受托责任履行情况以及报告使用者决策或者监督、管理的需要相关，有助于报告使用者对政府会计主体过去、现在或者未来的情况作出评价或者预测。

第十四条　政府会计主体对已经发生的经济业务或者事项，应当及时进行会计核算，不得提前或者延后。

第十五条　政府会计主体提供的会计信息应当具有可比性。

同一政府会计主体不同时期发生的相同或者相似的经济业务或者事项，应当采用一致的会计政策，不得随意变更。确需变更的，应当将变更的内容、理由及其影响在附注中予以说明。

不同政府会计主体发生的相同或者相似的经济业务或者事项，应当采用一致的会计政策，确保政府会计信息口径一致，相互可比。

第十六条　政府会计主体提供的会计信息应当清晰明了，便于报告使用者理解和使用。

第十七条　政府会计主体应当按照经济业务或者事项的经济实质进行会计核算，不限于以经济业务或者事项的法律形式为依据。

第三章　政府预算会计要素

第十八条　政府预算会计要素包括预算收入、预算支出与预算结余。

第十九条　预算收入是指政府会计主体在预算年度内依法取得的并纳入预算管理的现金流入。

第二十条　预算收入一般在实际收到时予以确认，以实际收到的金额计量。

第二十一条　预算支出是指政府会计主体在预算年度内依法发生并纳入预算管理的现金流出。

第二十二条　预算支出一般在实际支付时予以确认，以实际支付的金额计量。

第二十三条　预算结余是指政府会计主体预算年度内预算收入扣除预算支出后的资金余额，以及历年滚存的资金余额。

第二十四条　预算结余包括结余资金和结转资金。

结余资金是指年度预算执行终了，预算收入实际完成数扣除预算支出和结转资金后剩余的资金。

结转资金是指预算安排项目的支出年终尚未执行完毕或者因故未执行，且下年需要按原用途继续使用的资金。

第二十五条　符合预算收入、预算支出和预算结余定义及其确认条件的项目应当列入政府决算报表。

第四章　政府财务会计要素

第二十六条　政府财务会计要素包括资产、负债、净资产、收入和费用。

第一节　资产

第二十七条　资产是指政府会计主体过去的经济业务或者事项形成的，由政府会计主体控制的，预期能够产生服务潜力或者带来经济利益流入的经济资源。

服务潜力是指政府会计主体利用资产提供公共产品和服务以履行政府职能的潜在能力。

经济利益流入表现为现金及现金等价物的流入，或者现金及现金等价物流出的减少。

第二十八条　政府会计主体的资产按照流动性，分为流动资产和非流动资产。

流动资产是指预计在1年内（含1年）耗用或者可以变现的资产，包括货币资金、短期投资、应收及预付款项、存货等。

非流动资产是指流动资产以外的资产，包括固定资产、在建工程、无形资产、长期投资、公共基础设施、政府储备资产、文物文化资产、保障性住房和自然资源资产等。

第二十九条　符合本准则第二十七条规定的资产定义的经济资源，在同时满足以下条件时，确认为资产：

（一）与该经济资源相关的服务潜力很可能实现或者经济利益很可能流入政府会计主体；

（二）该经济资源的成本或者价值能够可靠地计量。

第三十条　资产的计量属性主要包括历史成本、重置成本、现值、公允价值和名义金额。

在历史成本计量下，资产按照取得时支付的现金金额或者支付对价的公允价值计量。

在重置成本计量下，资产按照现在购买相同或者相似资产所需支付的现金金额计量。

在现值计量下，资产按照预计从其持续使用和最终处置中所产生的未来净现金流入量的折现金额计量。

在公允价值计量下，资产按照市场参与者在计量日发生的有序交易中，出售资产所能收到的价格计量。

无法采用上述计量属性的，采用名义金额（即人民币1元）计量。

第三十一条　政府会计主体在对资产进行计量时，一般应当采用历史成本。

采用重置成本、现值、公允价值计量的，应当保证所确定的资产金额能够持续、可靠计量。

第三十二条　符合资产定义和资产确认条件的项目，应当列入资产负债表。

第二节　负债

第三十三条　负债是指政府会计主体过去的经济业务或者事项形成的，预期会导致经济资源流出政府会计主体的现时义务。

现时义务是指政府会计主体在现行条件下已承担的义务。未来发生的经济业务或者事项形成的义务不属于现时义务，不应当确认为负债。

第三十四条　政府会计主体的负债按照流动性，分为流动负债和非流动负债。

流动负债是指预计在1年内（含1年）偿还的负债，包括应付及预收款项、应付职工薪酬、应缴款项等。

非流动负债是指流动负债以外的负债，包括长期应付款、应付政府债券和政府依法担保形成的债务等。

第三十五条　符合本准则第三十三条规定的负债定义的义务，在同时满足以下条件时，确认为负债：

（一）履行该义务很可能导致含有服务潜力或者经济利益的经济资源流出政府会计主体；

（二）该义务的金额能够可靠地计量。

第三十六条　负债的计量属性主要包括历史成本、现值和公允价值。

在历史成本计量下，负债按照因承担现时义务而实际收到的款项或者资产的金额，或者承担现时义务的合同金额，或者按照为偿还负债预期需要支付的现金计量。

在现值计量下，负债按照预计期限内需要偿还的未来净现金流出量的折现金额计量。

在公允价值计量下，负债按照市场参与者在计量日发生的有序交易中，转移负债所需支付的价格计量。

第三十七条　政府会计主体在对负债进行计量时，一般应当采用历史成本。

采用现值、公允价值计量的，应当保证所确定的负债金额能够持续、可靠计量。

第三十八条　符合负债定义和负债确认条件的项目，应当列入资产负债表。

第三节　净资产

第三十九条　净资产是指政府会计主体资产扣除负债后的净额。

第四十条　净资产金额取决于资产和负债的计量。

第四十一条　净资产项目应当列入资产负债表。

第四节　收入

第四十二条　收入是指报告期内导致政府会计主体净资产增加的、含有服务潜力或者经济利益的经济资源的流入。

第四十三条　收入的确认应当同时满足以下条件：

（一）与收入相关的含有服务潜力或者经济利益的经济资源很可能流入政府会计主体；

（二）含有服务潜力或者经济利益的经济资源流入会导致政府会计主体资产增加或者负债减少；

（三）流入金额能够可靠地计量。

第四十四条　符合收入定义和收入确认条件的项目，应当列入收入费用表。

第五节　费用

第四十五条　费用是指报告期内导致政府会计主体净资产减少的、含有服务潜力或者经济利益的经济资源的流出。

第四十六条　费用的确认应当同时满足以下条件：

（一）与费用相关的含有服务潜力或者经济利益的经济资源很可能流出政府会计主体；

（二）含有服务潜力或者经济利益的经济资源流出会导致政府会计主体资产减少或者负债增加；

（三）流出金额能够可靠地计量。

第四十七条　符合费用定义和费用确认条件的项目，应当列入收入费用表。

第五章　政府决算报告和财务报告

第四十八条　政府决算报告是综合反映政府会计主体年度预算收支执行结果的文件。

政府决算报告应当包括决算报表和其他应当在决算报告中反映的相关信息和资料。

政府决算报告的具体内容及编制要求等，由财政部另行规定。

第四十九条　政府财务报告是反映政府会计主体某一特定日期的财务状况和某一会计期间的运行情况和现金流量等信息的文件。

政府财务报告应当包括财务报表和其他应当在财务报告中披露的相关信息和资料。

第五十条　政府财务报告包括政府综合财务报告和政府部门财务报告。

政府综合财务报告是指由政府财政部门编制的，反映各级政府整体财务状况、运行情况和财政中长期可持续性的报告。

政府部门财务报告是指政府各部门、各单位按规定编制的财务报告。

第五十一条　财务报表是对政府会计主体财务状况、运行情况和现金流量等信息的结构性表述。

财务报表包括会计报表和附注。

会计报表至少应当包括资产负债表、收入费用表和现金流量表。

政府会计主体应当根据相关规定编制合并财务报表。

第五十二条　资产负债表是反映政府会计主体在某一特定日期的财务状况的报表。

第五十三条　收入费用表是反映政府会计主体在一定会计期间运行情况的报表。

第五十四条　现金流量表是反映政府会计主体在一定会计期间现金及现金等价物流

入和流出情况的报表。

第五十五条　附注是对在资产负债表、收入费用表、现金流量表等报表中列示项目所作的进一步说明，以及对未能在这些报表中列示项目的说明。

第五十六条　政府决算报告的编制主要以收付实现制为基础，以预算会计核算生成的数据为准。

政府财务报告的编制主要以权责发生制为基础，以财务会计核算生成的数据为准。

第六章　附则

第五十七条　本准则所称会计核算，包括会计确认、计量、记录和报告各个环节，涵盖填制会计凭证、登记会计账簿、编制报告全过程。

第五十八条　本准则所称预算会计，是指以收付实现制为基础对政府会计主体预算执行过程中发生的全部收入和全部支出进行会计核算，主要反映和监督预算收支执行情况的会计。

第五十九条　本准则所称财务会计，是指以权责发生制为基础对政府会计主体发生的各项经济业务或者事项进行会计核算，主要反映和监督政府会计主体财务状况、运行情况和现金流量等的会计。

第六十条　本准则所称收付实现制，是指以现金的实际收付为标志来确定本期收入和支出的会计核算基础。凡在当期实际收到的现金收入和支出，均应作为当期的收入和支出；凡是不属于当期的现金收入和支出，均不应当作为当期的收入和支出。

第六十一条　本准则所称权责发生制，是指以取得收取款项的权利或支付款项的义务为标志来确定本期收入和费用的会计核算基础。凡是当期已经实现的收入和已经发生的或应当负担的费用，不论款项是否收付，都应当作为当期的收入和费用；凡是不属于当期的收入和费用，即使款项已在当期收付，也不应当作为当期的收入和费用。

第六十二条　本准则自 2017 年 1 月 1 日起施行。

资料来源：http：//tfs. mof. gov. cn/zhengwuxinxi/caizhengbuling/201511/t20151102_1536662. html。

附录4　国际会计准则理事会发布的主要准则

国际会计准则理事会（International Accounting Standards Board，IASB）旨在制订高质量、易于理解和具可行性的国际会计准则，准则要求向公众披露的财务报告应具明晰性和可比性。国际证监会组织（IOSCO）、国际会计师联合会（IFAC）、世界银行（World Bank）、国际货币基金组织（IMF）、经济合作与发展组织（OECD）、八国集团（Group of Eight）、巴塞尔银行监管委员会（BCBS）、国际审计和鉴证准则理事会（IAASB）等都相继发表声明，认可 IASB 作为全球会计准则的制定主体所做的努力，支持国际会计准则的建设。此外，IASB 还联手各国的国家会计准则制订者在国际准则的制订上达成一致。

国际会计准则不具有法律性质，各国是否遵循它，取决于在各国看来是否有利于该国或是否有条件实施，IASB 不能强制某国遵循国际会计准则，尽管如此，随着跨国经济的发展和国际资本的逐步完善，以 IASs/IFRSs 为主体的会计标准体系正在赢得全球会计准则的地位，会计准则趋同是当今会计国际协调的现实选择，也是大势所趋。以下列出现行有效的国际会计准则（International Accounting Standards，IASs）和国际财务报告准则（International Financial Reporting Standards，IFRSs）。

IAS 1 Presentation of Financial Statements　国际财务报告准则第 13 号——财务报表列报

IAS 2 Inventories　国际会计准则第 2 号——存货

IAS 7 Statement of Cash Flows　国际会计准则第 7 号——现金流量表

IAS 8 Accounting Policies，Changes in Accounting Estimates and Errors　国际会计准则第 8 号——会计政策、会计估计变更和差错

IAS 10 Events after the Reporting Period　国际会计准则第 10 号——资产负债表日后事项

IAS 12 Income Taxes　国际会计准则第 12 号——所得税

IAS 16 Property，Plant and Equipment　国际会计准则第 16 号——不动产、厂房和设备

IAS 19 Employee Benefits　国际会计准则第 19 号——雇员福利

IAS 20 Accounting for Government Grants and Disclosure of Government Assistance　国际会计准则第 20 号——政府补助金会计和政府援助的披露

IAS 21 The Effects of Changes in Foreign Exchange Rates　国际会计准则第21 号——外汇汇率变动的影响

IAS 23 Borrowing Costs 国际会计准则第 23 号——借款费用

IAS 24 Related Party Disclosures 国际会计准则第 24 号——关联方披露

IAS 26 Accounting and Reporting by Retirement Benefit Plans 国际会计准则第 26 号——退休福利计划的会计和报告

IAS 27 Separate Financial Statements 国际会计准则第 27 号——单独财务报表

IAS 28 Investments in Associates and Joint Ventures 国际会计准则第 28 号——在联营企业和合营企业中的投资

IAS 29 Financial Reporting in Hyperinflationary Economies 国际会计准则第 29 号——恶性通货膨胀经济中的财务报告

IAS 32 Financial Instruments：Presentation 国际会计准则第 32 号——金融工具：列报

IAS 33 Earnings per Share 国际会计准则第 33 号——每股收益

IAS 34 Interim Financial Reporting 国际会计准则第 34 号——中期财务报告

IAS 36 Impairment of Assets 国际会计准则第 36 号——资产减值

IAS 37 Provisions，Contingent Liabilities and Contingent Assets 国际会计准则第 37 号——准备、或有负债和或有资产

IAS 38 Intangible Assets 国际会计准则第 38 号——无形资产

IAS 40 Investment Property 国际会计准则第 40 号——投资性房地产

IAS 41 Agriculture 国际会计准则第 41 号——农业

IFRS 1 First-time Adoption of International Financial Reporting Standards 国际财务报告准则第 1 号——首次采用国际财务报告准则

IFRS 2 Share-based Payment 国际财务报告准则第 2 号——以股份为基础的支付

IFRS 3 Business Combinations 国际财务报告准则第 3 号——企业合并

IFRS 5 Non-current Assets Held for Sale and Discontinued Operations 国际财务报告准则第 5 号——持有待售的非流动资产和终止经营

IFRS 6 Exploration for and Evaluation of Mineral Resources 国际财务报告准则第 6 号——矿产资源的勘探和评估

IFRS 7 Financial Instruments：Disclosures 国际财务报告准则第 7 号——金融工具：披露

IFRS 8 Operating Segments 国际财务报告准则第 8 号——经营分部

IFRS 9 Financial Instruments 国际财务报告准则第 9 号——金融工具

IFRS 10 Consolidated Financial Statements 国际财务报告准则第 10 号——合并财务报表

IFRS 11 Joint Arrangements 国际财务报告准则第 11 号——合营安排

IFRS 12 Disclosure of Interests in Other Entities 国际财务报告准则第 12 号——其他主体中权益的披露

IFRS 13 Fair Value Measurement 国际财务报告准则第13号——公允价值计量

IFRS 14 Regulatory Deferral Accounts 国际财务报告准则第14号——递延账户监管

IFRS 15 Revenue from Contracts with Customers 国际财务报告准则第15号——与客户之间的合同产生的收入

IFRS 16 Leases 国际财务报告准则第16号——租赁

IFRS 17 Insurance Contracts 国际财务报告准则第13号——保险合同

资料来源：https：//www. ifrs. org/groups/international-accounting-standards-board/#about。

附录 5　致力于国际会计协调的国际组织

任何一个国家都不能孤立于世界经济之外，在这种情况下，国际间的贸易越来越发展，越来越扩大，会计的国际协调化对发展国际贸易来说具有很大的促进作用。国际会计协调是通过各种国际性政府间机构、区域性国家联盟、官方机构国际组织以及会计职业界的民间国际组织或专设机构来推动的，它们的努力和共同合作，在不同领域和不同程度上取得了重大的成果。现就其中几个致力于国际会计协调的国际组织做一个简单介绍。

一、国际会计准则理事会（International Accounting Standards Board，IASB）

IASB 是由国际财务报告准则基金会（IFRS Foundation）设立的独立的会计准则制定机构，成立于 2001 年，总部设在英国伦敦。IASB 的前身是国际会计准则委员会（International Accounting Standards Committee，简称 IASC）。

IASB 负责制定及批准国际财务会计报告准则、解释委员会公告，在 IFRS Foundation 的监督下工作。IASB 旨在制订高质量、易于理解和可实施的国际会计准则，该准则要求向公众披露的财务报告应具明晰性和可比性。目前 IASB 拥有在会计准则制定、会计教育等领域经验丰富的 14 名理事，由 IFRS Foundation 任命。其中有一名来自中国的理事。

二、国际会计师联合会（The International Federation of Accountants，IFAC）

IFAC 成立于 1977 年，是会计行业的国际组织，总部位于美国纽约。IFAC 由 130 多个国家和地区的 175 个成员组织和准成员组织组成，代表着全球近 300 万在事务所、教育、政府和工商业等领域工作的职业会计师。

IFAC 的宗旨是服务于公众利益并强化会计行业，为此，IFAC 致力于制定高质量的国际职业准则（包括国际审计准则、国际会计教育准则、国际会计师职业道德守则，以及国际公共部门会计准则等），引导、推动其采用和实施，推动会计职业组织的能力建设，提升会计师的职业价值，以及在涉及公众利益的问题上代表全球会计行业发声。中国注册会计师协会于 1997 年 5 月 8 日加入 IFAC，并派代表担任理事。

三、国际会计和报告准则政府间专家工作组（Intergovernmental Working Group of Experts on International Standards of Accounting and Reporting，ISAR）

ISAR 由联合国经济社会理事会（ECOSOC）于 1982 年创立，是致力于企业层面的透明度及会计问题的政府间工作组。ISAR 通过研究、政府间对话、建立共识以及技术合作的综合方案来完成其任务。中国财政部和中注协派有代表参加工作组的工作。

ISAR 关注企业会计及报告方面的许多问题，以期提高公司报告的全球可比性和可靠性。主要任务是：对国家和地区层面的准则制定作出积极贡献；采取适当的行动以确保跨国公司披露的可比性；跟踪国际会计和报告领域的发展情况，包括各准则制定机构的工作；就国际会计和报告准则的制定向相关国际机构提供咨询，并征集各方的意见；作为国际机构考虑投资、技术及相关财务问题委员会的工作范围之内的会计和报告问题，以提升跨国公司披露信息的可及性和可比性；等等。

四、全球报告倡议组织（Global Reporting Initiative，GRI）

GRI 成立于 1997 年，由环境责任经济体同盟（Coalition for Environmentally Responsible Economies，CERES）和美国泰勒斯研究学院（Tellus）共同发起成立的独立的国际组织，其秘书处设在荷兰的阿姆斯特丹。

GRI 致力于推动企业、政府部门及其他机构提供可持续发展报告，帮助他们了解其行为对包括气候变化在内的重大可持续问题的影响，促进全球经济可持续发展。同时通过发布准则，将可持续发展作为机构决策的一个重要部分。

近年来，GRI 对其组织架构进行了改革。为了增强制定可持续发展报告准则工作的独立性，GRI 成立了全球可持续发展准则理事会（Global Sustainability Standards Board，GSSB），在 GRI 董事会的支持下，作为独立运营的机构，以服务于公众利益为宗旨，承担制定可持续发展报告准则的职责。目前，GSSB 制定有可持续发展报告准则 G4 版。

五、全球会计联盟（Global Accounting Alliance，GAA）

GAA 于 2005 年 11 月成立。GAA 的宗旨是通过与各成员组织共享信息，就全球会计领域重要问题开展沟通与合作，推动会计行业为公众提供高质量的专业服务。近年来，GAA 致力于通过其成员组织，加强与各个国家和地区政府部门、监管机构及相关团体的联系沟通，就全球经济发展中的重大问题发表看法，提出会计职业界的意见和建议。

GAA 由来自美国、加拿大、澳大利亚、新西兰、英国、德国、日本、南非、爱尔兰等国家，和我国香港特别行政区的 10 个会计职业组织组成，其理事会由各成员组织首席执行官组成。

六、亚太会计师联合会（The Confederation of Asian and Pacific Accountants，CAPA）

CAPA 是亚太地区各会计职业组织组成的地区性机构，成立的最初构想始于 1957 年 12 月 1 日在菲律宾马尼拉召开的第一次远东会计师大会。CAPA 正式成立于 1976 年，其秘书处设于马来西亚吉隆坡。迄今为止，CAPA 是世界上覆盖地域最大的区域会计职业组织，覆盖全球一半的区域。目前，CAPA 拥有来自亚洲、大洋洲和太平洋沿岸 23 个国家和地区的 33 个会计职业组织会员。

CAPA 的宗旨是：在亚太地区会计行业的发展、提高和协调方面发挥领导作用，使会计行业能够不断为社会公众提供高质量的服务。CAPA 的决策机构是理事会，负责实现 CAPA 目标的具体工作，每年召开两次会议。理事会每四年选举一次，由不超过 12 名成员组成，所有成员应为不同地区正式会员组织所授权的代表。CAPA 主席和副主席由理事会选举产生，任期各为两年。理事会设治理与审计委员会、职业会计组织发展委员会（PAODC）及公共部门财务管理委员会（PSFMC）。

七、亚洲—大洋洲会计准则制定机构组织（Asian - Oceanian Standard - Setters Group，AOSSG）

AOSSG 由亚洲、大洋洲地区会计准则制定机构组成，该组织成立的目的是探讨有关采用国际财务报告准则（IFRS）的问题并分享经验，并为制定高质量的全球会计准则做出贡献。AOSSG 旨在鼓励在该地区采用国际财务报告准则方面发挥重要作用，目前共有来自 26 个国家和地区的 26 家成员组织。

AOSSG 的目标是：促进本地区各国采用国际财务报告准则并与之相趋同；促进本地区各国持续实施国际财务报告准则；协调本地区参与国际会计准则理事会（IASB）技术性工作；与各国政府和监管机构以及其他区域和国际组织合作，以提高本地区的财务报告质量。

八、特许公认会计师公会（The Association of Chartered Certified Accountants，ACCA）

ACCA 的前身伦敦会计师公会（London Association of Accountants）成立于 1904 年，至 1984 年正式更名为 ACCA。ACCA 总部设在伦敦，在全球设有 95 家办事处。目前拥有 200 000 名会员和 486 000 名学员，分布在全球 180 多个国家和地区。

ACCA 的管理机构为理事会，由全球会员选举产生的 36 名理事以及 1 名指定成员组成。理事会选举产生会长、侯任会长及副会长，并任命执行总裁。理事会下设若干委员会，包括提名委员会、惩戒委员会、申诉委员会、招生许可委员会等。执行团队是 ACCA 主要决策机构，由 1 名执行总裁、3 名执行总监和 2 名顾问组成。

九、国际会计师公会（The Association of International Accountants，AIA）

AIA 成立于 1928 年，总部设在英国，是一家国际性会计专业考试机构和会员团体，其专业资格证书受到英国政府的官方认可，会员分布在全球 80 个国家和地区。

国际会计师公会的主要目标是：成为职业会计师的国际化组织；通过教育培训，推广国际会计准则、国际审计准则、职业道德标准及国际商务管理和实践，支持会计行业的国际趋同；为国际会计师公会所在国家和地区的会计行业提供支持和协作。

十、泛非洲地区会计师联合会（Pan - African Federation of Accountants，PAFA）

PAFA 是代表非洲地区会计职业组织的机构，成立于 2011 年，是一家非政府组织。其使命是代表泛非洲地区会计职业的声音，推动其服务于公众利益、促进贸易、为成员组织国家提供高质量服务的能力。该联合会现有来自包括博茨瓦纳、刚果、尼日利亚、赞比亚等 43 个国家的 50 余家会计职业组织成员，个人会员 11 万余人。

资料来源：http：//www. cicpa. org. cn/intercommunication/professional_organizations/.

主要参考文献

［1］贺欣，温倩，罗殿英：《会计审计专业英语》，机械工业出版社 2019 年版。

［2］张捷：《基础会计》，中国人民大学出版社 2018 年版。

［3］陈艳利：《会计学基础》，高等教育出版社 2017 年版。

［4］高顿财经研究院：《Financial Accounting》，高等教育出版社 2017 年版。

［5］Bazley Nikolai Jones，余恕莲改编：《Intermediate Accounting》，高等教育出版社 2016 年版。

［6］Carl S. Warren，叶陈刚改编：《Survey of Accounting》，高等教育出版社 2015 年版。

［7］郭葆春：《会计专业英语》，中国人民大学出版社 2013 年版。

［8］王善平，唐红：《国际会计学》，东北财经大学出版社 2013 年版。

［9］叶建芳等：《会计英语》，东北财经大学出版社 2011 年版。

［10］孙坤：《会计英语》，东北财经大学出版社 2008 年版。

［11］李越冬：《会计英语简明教程》，西南财经大学出版社 2005 年版。